"Imani Perry wants her young sons 'to make beauty and love in a genocidal time.' Bless them! And bless her, for this book is a wonderful model for doing just that! So much joy and caring and pain and rage distilled into soaring, striking sentences."

—AMITAVA KUMAR, author of *Immigrant, Montana*

"*Breathe* is a masterpiece. With an approach that is at once vulnerable and brave, scholarly and artistic, critical and hopeful, Imani Perry has written the book that we desperately need. *Breathe* arms us with the wisdom, courage, and hope necessary to parent Black children within a White supremacist world. *Breathe* not only demonstrates Perry's deep love of her sons but also her profound and abiding faith in the rich traditions, ambitious freedom dreams, and boundless possibilities of Black people. This is an offering of profound beauty and brilliance that marks Imani Perry's emergence as the leading writer and thinker of this generation."

—MARC LAMONT HILL

"Before reading *Breathe*, I knew that Imani Perry was the most important cultural worker in my professional life. But I had no idea that Imani Perry, or any writer in this country, could pull off what she pulls off in *Breathe*. More than any book I've read in the last twenty years, *Breathe* boldly reminds us that artful intentionality is not nearly as important as artful effectiveness, and artful effectiveness is shaped by the love a writer has for her intended audience. Somehow, Perry manages to mourn, celebrate, theorize, and welcome us into the space between, and around, this Black mother and her Black sons. Though the language here is different from all of Perry's other work, the attentiveness to sustained analysis is even more apparent. One feels that Perry had to write her other five books to write this one, the smallest and ironically the most rigorous, personal, and soulful of all of her genius work. *Breathe* is the first book I've ever needed to read out loud with my mother."

—KIESE LAYMON, author of *Heavy: An American Memoir*

"There are moments when a piece of writing is so honest, so personal, that it crawls into us. Moments when words attach themselves to instances in our pasts, visions of our futures, or the purgatorial questions of today. *Breathe* is that. Perry gives us a look into what it means to love her children—her Black sons—in a world that may not. What it means to arm them with information, history, culture, spirit, pride, and joy. What it means to celebrate with them the vastness of their lineage and the tight network of community, which affords them an impenetrable freedom to be. To just . . . be. And as Perry gives this to her sons—her family—with such candor and respect, I couldn't help but hear my own mother speaking her truth, our truth, to me."

—JASON REYNOLDS, Newbury Award honoree and author of the Track series, *Ghost*, *Patina*, *Sunny*, and *Lu*

"*Breathe* is at once a resplendent meditation on the labor and art of parenting and on the 'special calling' of mothering Black boys in America. By turns fierce and loving, intimate and erudite, and drawing with deep complexity on her Catholic theology and spirituality, Imani Perry interweaves the most universal of dreams and desires with the particular traumas of our world of 'wild-eyed' whiteness. In so doing she offers her sons—and all the rest of us, and our sons and daughters—a vision of human resilience and wholeness that could reframe and redeem this young century's painful reckonings."

—KRISTA TIPPETT, founder and CEO, The On Being Project, and curator, The Civil Conversations Project

Breathe

Breathe

A Letter to My Sons

IMANI PERRY

Beacon Press
BOSTON

BEACON PRESS
Boston, Massachusetts
www.beacon.org

Beacon Press books
are published under the auspices of
the Unitarian Universalist Association of Congregations.

22 21 20 19   8 7 6 5 4 3 2 1

This book is printed on acid-free paper that meets the uncoated
paper ANSI/NISO specifications for permanence as revised in 1992.

Text design and composition by Kim Arney

June Jordan, from "Poem About My Rights," from *We're On: A June Jordan Reader*
(Alice James Books, 2017) © 2017 June M. Jordan Literary Estate. Reprinted by
permission. www.junejordan.com. Excerpts from Gwendolyn Brooks's "The Life of
Lincoln West" and "Boy Breaking Glass" reprinted by consent of Brooks Permissions.

Library of Congress Cataloging-in-Publication Data

Names: Perry, Imani.
Title: Breathe : a letter to my sons / Imani Perry.
Description: Boston, Massachusetts : Beacon Press, 2019. |
Includes bibliographical references. |
Identifiers: LCCN 2019003863 (print) | LCCN 2019004378 (ebook) |
ISBN 9780807076569 (ebook) | ISBN 9780807076552 (hardback)
Subjects: LCSH: Perry, Imani | African American mothers—Biography. | African
American educators—Biography. | African American families. | African American
boys—Social conditions. | African Americans—Social conditions. | Racism—United
States. | United States—Race relations. | BISAC: BIOGRAPHY
& AUTOBIOGRAPHY / Personal Memoirs.
Classification: LCC E185.86 (ebook) | LCC E185.86 .P477 2019 (print) |
DDC 306.85/08996073—dc23
LC record available at https://lccn.loc.gov/2019003863

For the ancestors
and the children

Children imitating cormorants
Are even more wonderful
Than cormorants.

———

Even on the smallest islands,
They are tilling the fields
Skylarks singing.

—KOBAYASHI ISSA

Contents

Through good, nothing, or ill, your mother stands
behind you, in front of the looking glass.
The boy standing before his mother blinks.
And there is another, stalk high.
Seeing a child, and another
I know and do not know.
My own and belonging only to himself
and to himself.
Smuggling truth off the well-worn and decent corridors.
Mother to son, we race in the woods,
through an underground railroad of all ways.
Dear sons of cotton, muscle, and bone
I am for you.

Breathe

Fear

I am not wrong: Wrong is not my name
My name is my own my own my own
　—JUNE JORDAN[1]

It must be terrifying to raise a Black boy in America.
　—EVERYBODY AND THEIR MOTHER (AND FATHER TOO)

Between me and these others—who utter the sentence—
the indelicate assertion hangs mid-air. Without hesitation, they speculate as if it is a statement of fact. I look into their wide eyes. I see them hungry for my suffering, or crude with sympathy, or grateful they are not in such a circumstance. Sometimes they are even curious. It makes my blood boil, my mind furnace-hot. I seldom answer a word.

I am indignant at their pitying eyes. I do not want to be their emotional spectacle. I want them to admit that you are people. Black boys. People. This fact, simple as it is, shouldn't linger on the surface. It should penetrate. It often doesn't. Not in this country anyway.

But no matter how many say so, my sons, you are not a problem. Mothering you is not a problem. It is a gift. A vast one. A breathtaking one, beautiful. One that makes me pray for an unmercenary spirit about what I am here to do, never considering it a burden or worthy of particular praise. Mema, your grandmother, said it this way, "Mothering Black boys in America—that is a special calling."

How do I meet it? What is it like?

How do I meet this calling? Is it like cultivating diamonds? Pressure that is so tight that it turns you, Black, into something white and shiny and deemed precious and valuable? That is no good. Do I fuel it like coal, something that is to be burned up and used for the warmth of others? Or the consolation prize on Christmas? That's no good either.

Do I cover my home in the blood of a proverbial sacrificial goat, praying that we are passed over? That the blood-thirsty fear lands at someone else's door? I am tempted, but I know that prayers don't prevent tragedy; they hold you up as you pass through it. Sometimes.

Is it like stalking through a labyrinth, breathless yet deliberate, avoiding the snow-white minotaur? Maybe I am Theseus.

Was it ever so apparent that we need to have this reckoning?

Maybe I am Theseus. A living vocation, but also simply living with beckoning, and that is what it feels like. Its tenor and tone shift with the shadows of each day. But it is always there. Sometimes it screeches; sometimes it trills and warbles. Sometimes it is a perfect sweet pitch.

Sons,

I know you have heard about the abolitionist Sojourner Truth. She is slipped out of the pocket frequently for Black History Month bona fides. Her story is sparely told, a thousand times over, each day in February. Lacking potency even more than accuracy, the tellers make her, as you well know, both melodramatic and frankly boring. The truth is better.

In 1826, Truth, enslaved in New York, ran away from her captor. She was due to be freed by dint of the gradual emancipation statute. But she suspected her owner was trying to find ways to keep her. So, she got herself free. Two years later her son Peter, who was also due to be freed, was sold away to a plantation in Alabama in violation of the New York state statute. Truth, illiterate and Black, sued for Peter's return. And she won.

I have imagined her testimony. Imagined because we have no authentic record besides the fact that she always made listeners quake. The depth in her voice, the straightness of her spine. The ripple of terror and outrage. Her child was stolen. I imagine Peter, too, down south for the first time, facing rows of cotton. Maybe his fingers bled. Cotton is rough. Maybe he stood in a parallel row to one of our people—ones who had only had Alabama's cruelty. It could be that a grand of ours fashioned him a straw pallet. Made it extra plump to soften his fate. Fussed at him, "Boy, eat!" when he couldn't stop crying and snotting, mumbling in Dutch, missing his mama. Long miserable nights. Before, like a miracle, he got to go north. Back home.

So many mothers, many thousands more, never saw their children return. They witnessed only departures. Theft. Except perhaps on some private Pentecost, days full of unexpected grace in dreams, or in the afterlife. Or all three.

In the flesh, on the block they trembled. Buyers admired the evenness of form, the power. The things I admire: your sinewy strength, the eyes that tend towards vigilance. Beautiful to me, valuable for human thieves. Mothers like me once had no recourse. No power to hold off the lash, to hold on indefinitely, to fight back when they crushed your heart and life. I think back then I would have been like Frederick Douglass's mother. I would have bared one of my scars, like the one on my knee from a bit of flying charcoal at a cookout when I was six, and told you to remember me by it, in the crowd of endless labor, to know me by it. And if I didn't have a landmark on my flesh I would have made one for you, carved it into my right arm, a knifed "X" for your mother.

So, you know, this life we have is grace.

In the Catholic tradition, there is a form of grace—the sanctifying one—that is the stuff of your soul. It is not defined by moments of mercy or opportunity. It is not good things happening to you. Rather it is the good thing that is in you, regardless of what happens. You carry this down through generations, same as the epigenetic trauma of a violent slave master's society. But the grace is the bigger part. It is what made the ancestors hold on so that we could become.

And I have tried to make things just so in appreciation to them and for us.

Freeman Diallo. When I gave birth to you, I had labored for twenty-four hours. The first words ever said about you came from your father. "He's beautiful." They cut you out of me, a thin, wavering bloody line, and then my flesh stretched wide for you, and you were born brown mixed with red like the clay of the Black Belt. I had barely dilated, only a centimeter. Like I couldn't bear to let you go. And the obstetrician said that in another time in history I wouldn't have made it. Too small, too tight. Thank God you came into this world when you did. Thank God for the scalpel that broke you into this time.

My second delivery was quick. I had a planned C-section; I entered the surgical theater foggy and fifteen minutes later, Issa, you were in my arms. I saw no blood, no gore, and felt no pain until the next day when all of the medication wore off, and even then, the euphoria and endorphins of your freshness made the incision barely more painful than a bad scrape. You kept your eyes closed and your face was pink (pink!) and surrounded by little black curls. Your brother played on the cool tile hospital floor with a cardboard farm that housed tiny plastic animals. His cheeks were russet, chapped, and he was cheery for the sweet baby who, having claimed he was giving birth along with me, he called "Georgie Pickles." You were serene. The nurse said:

"I remember you. You were the one who tried to leave an hour after you had the baby last time." And laughed.

It's true. I had my baby and I was done with them, the institutionalized tile floors, the constant temperature taking, the rolling steel bassinet they put by my bedside—I just wanted you in my arms. I got my friend to sneak me a chicken biscuit to get my strength up and then starting scheming on my escape from the coldness of the ward.

The first time I tried, I had a bit of trouble nursing. The lactation consultant said that I would get the hang of it. I didn't. It was painful, and Freeman you screamed and balled up those little fists and I wept. It was too soon, and too much, to fail. One of the maternity ward nurses saw me. She quietly closed the door and whispered to me, "Do you want to give him a little formula?" I answered, conspiratorially, "Yes do you think I can?" Mmhm, she said. Just don't tell them. I remember the nurse's hair, kinky twists with a spiral curl at the bottom, and that tiny little bottle of cream-colored liquid. And so soon, you got something in your belly, and I got some lanolin cream. And by the next day, after that one little bottle, you were nursing just fine. I was learning to be a little bit easy. At least with some things.

On the third day of the second time, we went home. There were then two car seats, a lime green room, trimmed in white, pretty sheets, a fluffy bumper for when you rolled around, a fine ebony crib, and a matching daybed. Together, you were outfitted in the modern Western style. Just so. I didn't sew your curtains, but I matched them to the walls and the cartoon decals and the comforter and the alphabet rug I bought so that you would know letters as soon as your vision was clear.

And when you came home from the hospital I was filled with nostalgia. Each time, I attempted an approximation of my sweetest childhood memories. Memory is a time machine. You don't just recall; you conjure in it.

When your father and I bought the house, we checked for lead paint, anticipating babies. I remembered the signs from my childhood featuring a Black child, chalky Black with a white cast around his mouth, telling us do not eat paint chips no matter how sweet they tasted. Paint was a predatory desire. You came home to safety.

When you were little, I dressed you in crisp plaid shorts and matching red hoodies. Boat shoes sometimes, saddle oxfords others. For formal occasions there were smocked dress clothes and Eton suits. You looked so fresh, so lush, golden and bronze plump bodies inside crisp preppy packages. People stopped us to see the pretty babies.

You lived on a block that was shaded with a canopy of trees. It was exactly the memory I wanted to have never disappeared, for you. The older you get, however, the more things break, no matter how just so a parent wants to make it.

No matter how "just so" I have tried, and often failed, to make things, I have known from the very first day of each of your lives that I cannot guarantee your safety. That is the thing that the voyeurs want to drink in. That is why they make me so mad, really. Because the truth is it *is* frightening. But the fear is not the heart of the thing. The fear is what comes because your preciousness collides with the ways of the world. And then there is the battle against it, that all of us are forced to wage, because as Wole Soyinka said, "Let us simply observe that the assault on human dignity is one of the prime goals of the visitation of fear, a prelude to the domination of the mind and the triumph of power."[2] So, like many others, I try to unravel the fear. And confront the rest.

The everyday. The homework, the cooking, the cleaning, the activities, the practices, the friends, the rearing, it is so much—even, or perhaps because of, the choices and things I have been afforded. And then, on top of that, the daily work of beating back the ugliness. And reconciliation with the irreconcilable. You live in some worlds that are more white than Black. And so, you learn, early on, that the aversion to Blackness can turn perfectly lovely people grotesque. Like in high school, for me. There was a brilliant teacher. He wore a military precision haircut in gray, and had piercing blue eyes, and a great deal of flourish. He yelled at me my first day, because I had forgotten to bring a pencil. He mocked my answers in class. He called me the names of other Black students. He openly disparaged the inclusion of Black authors in the curriculum after we, students, had insisted. He lied on my evaluations and said I hadn't turned in papers. He was beloved by my peers. He was a brilliant teacher, for whites only. The bifurcation of my experience, and that of my peers, in which they witnessed my humiliation, felt uncomfortable for them. They were disciplined into passive acceptance, into reaping the rewards, while I was humiliated over and over again. Ask a white person about these moments and often the veil falls. Their moral turpitude lies naked and ashamed. Bewildered at the idea that they might have something asked of them to disrupt the hideous truth. This is what you are surrounded by. Silent witnesses.

Liberals, the "good guys," of all stripes gnash their teeth at such truths, and smiles turn to bitter curls, which makes them ever more dangerous. This problem dwarfs partisanship and smug decency. It is constitutional.

I mean. As babies, you smelled of honey and powder. Your eyes glisten, your smiles are sweet. Everybody loves you, how could they not? You are clever and kind boys. And beautiful—I mean you are truly beautiful, but you are also beautiful in the way people like to look at beautiful. And your language is so crisp—listen to those Black boys who know all of those vocabulary words! And still they pick: OK smart but . . . aggressive, distracted, distracting. Too mobile, too slow, too fast, inattentive. Why are you still in the bathroom? It takes you too long to pee. It takes you too long to remember this algorithm, this table. You hold the pencil too tight, you do not hold it tightly enough—the words come out more gray than black. You are just too black. Sniping. You should have said something when that other kid said something racist exactly right then in that moment when your world was spinning. You judged the child who said something racist too harshly afterwards as you reconstituted, they didn't mean it, you cannot defend yourself, you should not have defended yourself. You are not allowed to defend yourself! You keep moving too much. You talk too much, you don't share enough in class. Stop taking up for other people. You do not tell the truth; they cannot handle it when you tell them the truths about themselves.

So many little vicious things. So many big things.

You are second-generation integrators. So, I went through it too. Not incessantly, but enough to keep me from speaking in school for several years of my adolescence. A mocking teacher, who either grimaces at you or gives you a cruel smile, so covert as to claim constant innocence? Or one who simply cannot hear or see you? That's a strange and harrowing vulnerability. It makes you stoic when it is you. When it is your child? It is torture. And I am charged with holding back the torrent of my rage. I do it for you. I betray you so that the full fury of white supremacy with a currency of tears and accusations of insane black hypersensitive rage doesn't come down on you. I sin in order for you to survive. As Emily Dickinson said, I try to tell the truth but only tell it slant. And I am ashamed of that. Because the right thing to do, objectively speaking, would be to bless them out, call them everything but a child of God, offer them the pages and pages of evidence. I have studies and documents, and histories and examples, and I could drown them in their own indecency. Racism is in every step and every breath we take. It has been proven over and over again. But I don't. Most times. So that my love does not provide an excuse for more of their venom. Instead I teach you to read well. I teach you second sight—the word and also its meaning. The testament and the content. This is what is happening, I say. This is what they do. At first you are suspicious. My lessons are different from the official ones taught in every school: Everybody is friends. Everybody smiles. Everybody knows racism is bad. Nobody is racist because nobody is the Ku

Klux Klan around here. And the Ku Klux Klan is economically disenfranchised. Feel bad for them! And remember! If anyone white makes a mistake, they are INNOCENT. How dare you think otherwise? Trust me, says the wolf, with its canines gleaming. It is a threat, not an appeal.

Black lives matter. Brown lives matter. Lives in all the shapes they revile? Those matter too. There are deaths weekly. Children are stolen. Children are disappeared. We mourn, we rage. And then, beyond the tragedies you know have something to do with you, are the superseded things. In the stuff you are supposed to wipe off the corners of your mouth. Slights, shoves, pulled close to the body pocketbooks. Questions, never-ending questions about your abilities and quests to prove your inabilities. Resentment accrues when they fail. But they say you are the one with a bad attitude. Eventually you learn, most of the cries of innocence are bullshit. That you are always under the watchman's eye. Always presumed guilty, no matter how many smiles they give you. And I am sorry and proud at once. You have begun to understand your native land. The sacrament of this nation has become paper-thin life after the ugliest deaths, haunting and in the flesh. Perhaps we should bar mitzvah Black American boys at eleven. The book of Moses for which you are principally responsible would be Exodus. You would recite the blues, over and over until it is a moan, a growl, a mantra.

You were both little bits when President Obama was elected. That night was jubilant. We celebrated with friends, then, on the ride home, Black people cheered and danced in the streets. It reminded me of the night when Harold Washington won as mayor of Chicago, and strangers hugged me and my father. Such joy. It was a palate cleanse for a fragment of a moment. A season in which pundits speculated we might be postracial, in which scholars speculated that Black children would be less wounded; they called it a turning point, a point of no return. When Obama won, for a time Black tongues were scraped of bitterness and bile. Then the aftertaste came back like an earthquake.

Troy Davis. He was the first whose name you knew. Before either of you were born he witnessed a fight. A cop tried to break it up and was shot. And died. Troy Davis saw everything, but he insisted he wasn't the shooter. Someone else said he was.

The police were looking for Davis and so he turned himself in. Someone still said he did it, and there was a trial, and Davis was convicted. This was Georgia, a death penalty state. And Troy Davis was sentenced to death. His appeal for habeas relief—the potential grace note for unjust and unlawful detention—was denied.

Troy Davis became a household name because there were so many holes in the case. Seven witnesses recanted their (apparently coerced) testimonies. Eyewitnesses said it was his accuser and not Davis who did the shooting. The evidence of fabrication grew, and so did attention to Davis's plight. Archbishop Desmond Tutu and Pope Benedict both insisted on a halt to the killing machine. Former presidents and parliaments, even Republicans, implored. This man was innocent, and that fact was clear irrespective of what the court's procedures would recognize.

We went to demonstrations. We talked about the case. We joined the chorus pleading for Troy Davis's life. In the same way I was taught, I was teaching you how to think about injustice from an early age. No one understands fairness as much as young children. If you explain the way the world works, its pernicious efficacy, you will create justice warriors for a lifetime. They know what is right and wrong.

We sat together, me and you, Freeman, on that pretty pale-yellow denim couch. It wasn't stained yet from juice boxes and pizza. The night was September 20. You were up way past your bedtime. The news cameras covered the crowd outside the prison. The journalists told us what was happening inside, in that echoing lonely quiet. Troy Davis died at 11:08 p.m.

You looked at me, wide-eyed. "They killed him?"

They killed him. *They*. America. It. And whenever we forget and say the word *we*, it slices deep into our flesh. "Remember, nigger. Remember your place," is the national coda. I cried. You nestled in my arms. My poor child. You know intuitively that there are far more Troy Davises than Obamas. You are too smart for the surface jubilee to ever last. Sweet gets too sweet and turns bitter. It sticks and goes thick. Like cotton candy.

More protest. That was my first answer. That was what I knew to do. When I was a child and was prohibited from celebrating the Fourth of July (because, as Frederick Douglass asked, "What to the Slave is the Fourth of July?" and what is Independence Day to the oppressed?), I asked for a demonstration instead. The first time I was in the newspaper it was under a sign that read "Stop the War against Black America." I was much younger than five.

Something distinct has happened in your time. It is the product of camera phones, the diminishing whiteness of America, the backlash against a Black presidency, the persistence of American racism, the money-making weapons industry, the value added for murder in police dossiers, law-and-order policing. The epistrophe of our era: Hands up, don't shoot, can't breathe, can't run, can't play, can't drive, can't sleep, can't lose your mind unless you are ready to lose your life, dead dead dead. We wail and cry, how many pietàs? We protest their deaths; we protest for our lives.

Once our house alarm was tripped twice in one night. I tried to remain calm. But there was a loud banging sound at the back door the second time. The alarm company called again. I had said the police officers should not come the first time. I agreed the second time. You both were frightened. I was too. I called you, Freeman. Thank goodness you had a cell phone. I told you, softly, to lock your bedroom door and to not come out until I told you to. The first degree of fear, and I wonder at this, was not about the intruder who I thought was trying to get in. It was about the police, who I knew could get in, had a responsibility to get in, because they had been called.

I said lock your door because the possibility flashed before my face. You might be tipping out of your room, looking to come upstairs to me, or, in your breathtaking and youthful courage, looking to protect the home. And what if the police officers saw you, Mahogany in the shadows, tall and lean and dreadlocked, and decided you were the intruder, the one who didn't belong in this big house with lilac bushes and manicured Japanese trees in front? And what if they took you out?

There are fingers itching to have a reason to cage or even slaughter you. My God, what hate for beauty this world breeds. They say they are afraid. I do not believe it is fear. It is bloodlust.

People will say I'm being melodramatic. They have. But police kill middle-class Black children and adults too. Not with the same frequency, but class is no prevention. It is a reduction of the odds at best. As a Black mother, when I read about one of those children whose life has been snatched, at first blush I think, "That could have been my child." But I have demanded of myself that I turn away from such egotism. The truth is that is not my child. My children are here, and they stand with me, to honor their dead.

When Mamie Till shared the bloated distended face of her beautiful son Emmett, who was murdered, she did not offer other Black parents possession. Mamie Till's pietà was one in which she could not hold his wounded but still beautiful body across her lap. Hers was a pietà, instead, of distended, inflamed, and bloated remains from a distance; a pieta of a mother made empty-handed by virtue of the cruelty of the execution remains with us. That funeral service, a martyrdom, sending off a patron saint for those who survive after deaths, is an ever present haunting. I have not raised you in the church. Maybe that is a mistake. Faith helps us hold on. What do you do other than pray, an intercession not to bring the baby back, after all he is with God, but one to make stepping out of bed possible?

Mamie Till did it. She shared her testimony. Personal tragedy became the public's grief, one of so many during the freedom movement. Emmett's horrifyingly abused face resonated. Yet and still he was her baby and not the onlookers'. The same is true of the myriad who have followed. We witness private grief and feel it turn into our collective grief. But we must not snatch it up out of their loved ones' hearts and colonize it with our fears. Instead we stand in the chorus of mourners. I am sorry, Mrs. Till, Mrs. Fulton, Mr. Martin, Mrs. Davis, I am sorry we did not protect your child with every fiber of our beings. I am sorry we go on doing the same as yesterday while you collect the shards. It is not enough, but we will try to prevent the next. And we will fail. And our elegies grow reedy and more mournful. And our ache more confused and desperate. Ashen.

The ethics of living with a roulette wheel of Black death are complicated. "Sufficient unto the day is the evil thereof."[3] We do the fight today for the living. Grief must not be distorted into the constant imagination of death. We ward and guard and try to protect but know that there is no warding or guarding lest your whole life become their impunity.

When I stopped watching the killings, and declared it, people argued with me. They insisted that public executions would turn the tide. They were wrong. They just ratified the truth: summary execution is a feature of American life. Awareness is not a virtue in and of itself, not without a moral imperative. I knew the imperative wasn't there. I wanted to be wrong. But I wasn't. And I won't beat my chest, beat our minds to a bloody pulp in order to keep trying to have faith in a place that doesn't deserve it, in an American conscious-ness that hates more than it recognizes.

We cannot make of our lives a nightmarish *Fortnite* game with the guns cocked and ready for you as a target and our hands inexplicably empty of self-protection. Sons, I will not allow that to be your life. Your testimony is living with the passionate intensity of one whose presence matters de-spite the violence of this world towards your beautiful flesh.

Sufficient unto the day is the evil thereof. That is to say, we cannot even think about tomorrow; there is enough evil in this moment. Sufficient for each day is God's grace thereof, meaning I have the grace of your presence today. I have to hold on to that. "Finish each day and be done with it. You have done what you could. Some blunders and absurdities no doubt crept in; forget them as soon as you can. Tomorrow is a new day. You shall begin it serenely and with too high a spirit to be encumbered with your old nonsense," is what Emerson said.[4] But the truth is such haunting and trauma that I cannot help but ask the forward-looking questions.

How many pietàs? Holding the husk, praying for the spirit to have never departed. The life force escaped into a place that cannot be touched. Heart plummeted, this is what we do. Make me wanna holler, the way they do our lives. As Toni Cade Bambara said, "Those bones are not my child."[5] They are simply the remnants of a cruel world. The child has spread so vast that they become air and light, a thunderous rain, a sun shower, a rainbow.

Fairly soon, Issa, the protests became too much for you. You and your brother watched as we failed. We marched, we spoke out. We testified, we cried. And then there was another one, and another one. We lost, repeatedly. We watched conflagrations that burned into ashes and nothing was changed. The next day, or week, someone else was choked or shot in the back or stomped to death. Someone else encased in brown flesh like us. It was too much. No more marches; it made life too terrifying.

I had hoped that standing shoulder to shoulder with people of conscience, people who knew like us that the tocsin peal of Black death is wrong, would help you feel powerful, a part of something. I may have been right, but it was never enough.

When I took you down to the fiftieth anniversary of Freedom Summer, it was with a different sense of purpose. We flew to Jackson, Mississippi. I am always stunned that there is a state that feels so much like Alabama, like Mississippi does. Sound, taste, smell. Though most northerners treat the South as an undifferentiated mass, it is so specific, so local, so varied. But Alabama and Mississippi? They are twins, identical yet fed different diets, raised in different homes.

I would like to take you to Africa one day. I am one of those Black people who believes in the value of return. However, you have already been to your ancestral home many times. It is the Deep South. Of course, the further back you go, the bulk of ancestors were from a motley of West African peoples, a vast genetic variety, and some, as a consequence of rape, were from Europe. But the WE to which you belong was born in the South of the United States, though there were stops in the Caribbean and Maryland. Even New York was in there. The fact of becoming a people, to which you were born, happened on plantations. In slavery. I bristle when folks tell me that Black children should know their history didn't begin with slavery, as though slavery is shameful. Yes, of course, precolonial African history is important. Every child should have the fictions of imperialism aggressively bleached from their minds. Teach Songhay and Mali and Akan and Nubia. Stop narrowly constraining the idea of the classical and calling violent and vile conquest exploration. True. Yes. That's important. But I do not believe the acts of oppressors are my people's shame. For me, that my people became, created, and imagined from a position of unfreedom is a source of deep pride, not shame. I hope you learn that too. What better evidence of human beauty and resilience could there be?

And, if those genealogy tests are right, and that is a big if, when you trace your mother's mother's mother . . . far back as the sample can ride, it takes us back to an indigenous woman of the Americas. You are literally children of this place, from before it was a slaveholding settler-colonialist imperial country. You are survival. You have survived. We have.

I took you to Mississippi to catch a hold of who you are. I rented a car, an inexpensive one. The seats were plastic and the smell was just like my dad's old VW bug in which we rode through Alabama and sometimes down to Pensacola. We drove to the campus of Tougaloo, a historically Black college founded in 1869 to serve the educational aspirations of the freedpeople, fresh from slavery. It was where Anne Moody and Joyce Ladner, among other members of the Student Nonviolent Coordinating Committee, attended college. It was where the organizers rested at the end of the March Against Fear, the one that brought the call for Black Power to the center of the movement. And then, in 2014, it was where they chose to remember fifty years later, how Black youth changed the South and the nation.

Though you were seven and ten, you had already watched documentaries of the freedom movement. Issa, you said, wide-eyed, that you liked Professor Cleveland Sellers's overalls. He, a college president, wore a shirt and tie. He, a SNCC veteran, wore their workers' uniform. Poised, dignified, tall, lean. Past and present in one body. Everyman and exceptional man. I was hoping you saw some of that in yourself, a genealogy from whence you came, and where you might be going. How to remain.

In the gymnasium, Freeman, you sat transfixed as Mukasa Ricks preached from his memory, the story of his call and response with Stokely Carmichael, for Black Power. An elder, he bounded, his voice ricocheted, the spirit of a revolutionary had kept every bit of his energy youthful even as his body evidenced the years of struggle.

You both sat quietly, in the back of a classroom, to listen to the soft-spoken architect of Freedom Summer, Bob Moses. Glistening mahogany skin, a slow smile, and that riveting quiet intellect took over the room. He is your grandmother's friend, who you usually see on Martha's Vineyard with his wife, Miss Janet, playing with their grands. There you realized he was someone historic and both steely and soft.

On the campus there were organizers young and old. A pastor from Jamaica Plain, Massachusetts, by way of Arkansas, with a fedora on his head and dreadlocks hanging to his waist, sang the old-time blues, and a young eye-glassed short-locked dream defender from Florida and the second generation of hip-hop responded to his call with joy. There was love and legacy everywhere. And out of the fray, there were young men in orange jumpsuits. They trimmed hedges, cleaned walkways, labored steadily amongst the freedom fighters. They didn't catch our eyes. I noticed one with locks that hung to his wide shoulders. I saw his hands, broad and, at one moment, upturned as though pitifully empty. A prisoner among the freedom fighters, a human bellwether, a sacrificial lamb. There we all were, almost to a one, the descendants of slaves and croppers, and rapist slavers . . . and the Jim Crow rapists. Some literally held captive, some remembering a different form of captivity, some naming it all. And I think all of us knew that we hadn't yet realized the dreams of freedpeople who'd first settled down at Tougaloo.

I got lost on the way out of Mississippi. At one point we hit a dead-end road and my heart raced. An old man, leather-faced, overalled, with a cap on his head and gaunt sharp cheeks of a sort I've only seen in three places—the Dominican Republic, Louisiana, and Mississippi—led us out to the freeway. And we made our way home.

Driving from Jackson to Birmingham was easy. We ate donuts and listened to the scratchy radio, and 2014 felt like 1974 to me, except you were there, people I only dreamed of when I was little and playing with so many baby dolls. And that was the best feeling in the world.

I was born nine years after four little girls were killed in Birmingham, Alabama, and another, a boy, later the same day. On that trip, Auntie Thelma took us to Kelly Ingram Park. We circumambulated around the path, where the marchers had gathered, where the hoses and dogs lashed out at children, right in front of the Sixteenth Street Baptist Church, where the girls had died, across from the Civil Rights Institute, where the memories are held. The beating heart of Birmingham's freedom fighting.

The park is named after Osmond Kelly Ingram, a Navy man who was killed by Germans in World War I. He was the son of a Confederate veteran. Ingram senior devoted his life to keeping your ancestors bound to the evil of enslavement. That is not irony. That's the texture of our history. Every place is a battleground.

Kelly Ingram Park is quiet. The sculpture garden has the children behind bars, the clergy preaching freedom, the attacks on the people. It is so quiet and so vivid, cool dark metal statues surrounded by living green under a blazing hot Alabama sun. Not like a cemetery, better than most memorials because the haunting is visceral. You feel it when you stand close.

We walked around the sculptures, to the path converging in the center. There were children your sizes, I thought, who fought for you. For me. They fought for the ones in orange jumpsuits too.

An old man sitting on a park bench commented on your thick black curls, Freeman: "I used to have long pretty hair like that. But my daddy said he didn't want me to look like a sissy." My auntie thankfully shut him up. He wanted us to know he had been beautiful, and it made my chest hurt, because it was a belief that his beauty had something to do with looking a little bit less African, a little more Indian. He couldn't help but share a childhood hurt over an insecure masculinity, a cruel charge that beauty is gay and therefore somehow inferior. These things are things we have to grapple with, too, the ongoing work of trying to get free. There are parts to kill and parts to reincarnate, again and again.

You are gifted with something and it is important. You have seen Black men of every stripe, of every sort, for the entirety of your life. Famous and homeless. Athlete, intellectual, musician, teacher. Businessman, public servant, fast-food worker. Seen, and I do not mean simply knowing who they are, I mean hearing their stories. The range of dispositions and tones of laughter. Accents and nationalities and drawls and swagger and awkwardness. Hypermasculine and elegantly feminine and every variation in between. A common thread, a dramatic assortment. And you are members of this collaged confederacy, which, as a through line through all manner of circumstance, can share the Marvin Gaye refrain "Makes me wanna holler, the way they do my life . . . Makes me wanna holler, throw up both my hands."

In your own distinctive ways, you fit into the collective, even as there are moments when you may, by virtue of your rarefied circumstance, feel on its margins. I suppose that is why I have always insisted that you travel with me into the hood. Literally, the hood, as in the abbreviation for the neighborhood, as in the Blackest of spaces, also known as being all up in the cut. I'm talking about the ghetto. The word "hood" reverberates, pointed white, tall Klan hoods, and the businessmen and politicians underneath who carved out pyramids of exclusion and containment. The hoodies, a relatively cheap way to keep warm, to encase the body, to protect it, become narrative symbols for an undesired Blackness. "No hoodies allowed" the signs say, or they are simply justifications for trigger-happy police. The hood, the hoods. There is something about that word that speaks to our beating hearts. I want you to know it is with you even when you don't know it that well. You carry it like an invisible backpack. Of course they discern it, in the echo of your brown faces, but they do not see its riches, its resilience, in the carriage of your square shoulders. You must.

This is not some pat romanticism. Trust me. We do not want the trials of poverty. We do not want the wrecking ball instead of the hammer. That can only be a colonizer's fantasy. The province of those who want to eat up everything, even the suffering they create. But we know the story of Brer Rabbit. How he outwitted being punished for theft by begging, "Whatever you do, please don't throw me into the briar patch." And then, tossed there, he gleefully sang, "Born and bred in the briar patch." Don't be afraid of being cast with the briar patch. Know the bounty that is there. The lush forestation, the deep roots. The roping connections under the surface, that persist beyond life.

We cried for Trayvon. You heard every bit of how a child was made a demon. And hunted. A child like you. You wore hoodies as resistance, like a million more, innocent and beautiful, a target but more importantly an unapologetic human being. It was moving. And then it was heartbreaking.

I told you not to raise your hands up in the don't-shoot position that was common then. I told you to raise your right fists, how I was taught. Power.

The massacre happens in police violence. In hoods flooded with guns. In survivalists and antisocialists for whom murder gives purpose. This nation that is yours by inheritance and birth is in a state of panic and disaster. It's imperial grandeur is ending. Upward mobility is waning; precariousness is multiplying. And yet the rich keep getting richer. Whiteness is ebbing. And those who are afraid are turning to a game of cowboys and gangsters, going out with a viral blaze of glory. Children keep dying. The world keeps turning them bitter and demonic in deed.

My children. You have seen us, the adults in your world, impotent to bring our lost ones back, to protect the children or the mothers or the fathers, or to even avenge their deaths as useless as retribution would be when it comes to broken hearts. We have completely failed at making those who act with violent impunity stop what they're doing. In fact, a call to the police is an audaciously wielded weapon of white discontent these days. With each sin the violent hateful ones grow bolder. They know they can take our lives without consequence. And if not that, stage theaters of our humiliation. And yet, your power sustains.

My father had the poem "Who Killed McDuffie?" above his desk while I was growing up. It is a harrowing account of the unsolved murder of a Black man in Miami in 1979. I learned, practically from birth, that judicial procedure was a cruel choreography and not a fact finding when it came to violence against Black people. That is the terror that makes me want to say, "That could have been my child," and also, "That could have been me," even though thoughts of the self cannot, should not, take over our collective outrage and grief. And I know that, despite my fear, I cannot clip your wings, as though cowering is a respectful tribute to the beauty we have lost. No, I want your wingspan wide. To honor the departed, ancestral, and immediate—BE. Living defined by terror is itself destructive of the spirit. And it is submission. The truth is that life is unsafe. And genius, more often than not, remains unvalidated or, even worse, dormant. But joy, even in slivers, shows up everywhere. Take it. And keep taking it.

All that said, here is a strange truth: death and brutality can happen to any Black child, but the suffering is not distributed evenly. Police do not cruise through our neighborhood. You will not be harassed every day on your way home. Some days, yes, but not every day, not most days. With all of the borders you cross in this society, of race and class and state, you have not crossed a national border without papers, have not been stopped and declared a violator. It will probably first happen when you are driving. Or maybe on public transportation. Or maybe in a mall, some security person will follow you. But it will probably not happen every day of your life. You do not dwell in the playgrounds of repression, even though you are squarely in America. You stand on the outskirts of the tornado, where you can get sucked in, but where you might have a chance to take cover.

You are saved more than a few ravages, because of class and status, but you must understand that is an accident of birth and nothing more and develop your ethics accordingly. That is to say, don't believe the hype. You aren't "different" from other Negroes. You are in the middle and on the margins of this configuration of beauty and its repression. That is all. And I do not mean that you haven't dealt with difficult things. You have. You are human. And you will deal with many more, and yes they will have to do with Blackness often enough, though not exclusively. And more than that, you are Black in America, which means rage is your familiar, even if you haven't called it that yet. What I mean is, by virtue of where you live and go to school, and the possibility and comfort that are so often in your reach, you are not up close to the full weight of what Black life in America often is.

Remember once we went to a birthday party in North Philadelphia? We picked up the beautifully decorated cake from an Italian bakery on Fifth Street. We crowded into a small apartment. We drank Kool-Aid. We laughed, and you played. The language was different than the language at home, but it was a migrant's variation on the roots of Black English. I wondered that day, Did this feel as comfortable for you as for me? Did this feel safe? I wanted it to. I wanted it to feel like it could possibly be a refuge from the coldness of so many of the mostly white places that you found yourself. Maybe, maybe not. But you know this is a place to which you are bound, regardless. And if the little bit of advantage we cling onto slips out of our hands, it is a place you can go without being turned away.

Whether or not you ever have an intimate bond to any particular hood, it is inside you. It is yours. You cannot let the little modest spoils of capitalism's sorting hat confuse you. The landscape of your music and so much of your language lies there, a collage of past and present. An improvisation of dreams and their denial. We come from a common root—the grammar of the plantation, and before that of the continent, is yours and theirs. Think about it like this: The three of us have different tastes in music. But we all yearn for the feeling of bass in the chest that massages away rage. We all like a persistent beat. We all have tempers—sometimes in ways that defy the rules of being bourgeois. We yearn to curse people out. Issa, I knew it was true of you when you said to a little boy who thought your hair was a source of entertainment, "If you don't stop touching me, Imma drop you." That feeling, that reads to many as being "hard" in a manner that is specifically "hood," isn't artifice. It is something that courses through us like some epigenetic disposition. After centuries of humiliation and denigration, the hairs on our arms stand at attention each time the past is jogged in our present.

I wonder at the restraint our ancestors showed in order to survive with mouths and energies like ours. Perhaps they studied the discipline of the cool calm and collected Yoruba orisha, Obatala, the one who is like the Christian father—God—but hardly so patriarchal and political. Maybe they made selves inside, under the flesh, that could hold the anchor even as the storms knocked them down. Obatala is like the snail, and loves them, too, because no matter how hot the surroundings, the snail remains cool. I aspire to be like that, to teach you to be like that. But it is difficult. This world causes inflammation, and it flames.

You do not have to taste lead on your walls, breathe the environmental hazards of sick schools and buildings, pass through the metal detectors, stand under the daily gaze of cops. And still the toxins constantly threaten to seep under your skin and explode your insides outward, and like all Black people you must constantly drink the antidote. Every day, drink in the stories and the knowledge that teach you to refuse the pernicious myth that you are inferior. And not just of and about your own. Of all who have been desecrated and ground into nothingness. Refuse the lie. And when the antidote fails, hole yourself in a state of retreat, a cocoon of safety in which you can weep and rest.

Issa, we lost you when you were three years old. It was at a neighborhood fair. The most integrated area in Philadelphia was teeming with Black children. There were games and food and face painting and vendors. Water ice and funnel cake were special treats that you liked. We were wrapped in community. And then all of a sudden, you weren't there. The friend you were playing with was. But you were gone.

From birth we called you endearments. You learned you were precious in the informal intimate spaces, sobriquets as rootwork. "Issie, Is." Eight adults fanned out screaming every sweet variation of your name, looking for my baby. Minutes seemed like hours. And then, there you were. You stood alongside a police officer. But you didn't run to me. You looked at me, curiously. Because you weren't afraid.

And the officer almost wouldn't give you back. You had picked up a picture off the ground somewhere. It was of a Black man. And you handed it to the officer who reasonably assumed that was his parent. The officer was looking for the man in the picture, who looked nothing like either desperate parent in front of him. Thank goodness there were so many of us who had been calling your name to validate you were ours.

The feeling of failure is terrible. We had lost you. And you were not afraid. A success that was in fact a failure. You did not live with the taste of fear. Saving graces that kept that moment from swallowing me in shame? It was things like this: When the teachers asked you in preschool what you wanted to be when you grew up, you said happy. And when they asked what you were thankful for, you said your brother. And when they asked what made you happy now, you said it was when I made you special rice: saffron and curry, bright yellow with peas. I think that is what first got you to eat with a fork if I remember correctly.

You remember your play uncle? Uncle Byron? He knew how to have a good time. To laugh and be merry. And he held his cool in some of the most infuriating circumstances. When his brilliance was underestimated, when the world showed its canines at him and circumstance made him hold his fire.

Byron was a son of the Midwest. The Midwest is a place of the dream and its deferral. Byron was born in Missouri, a state of slavery and westward expansion. Once, when I asked him why St. Louis sold hot chips at the airport, he said, "Because they good like that and we hood like that." He was a poet, often sharing rhyming couplets on a weekly basis, clever and profound, and that too is a Midwestern gift. He was of a piece with Langston Hughes and Gwendolyn Brooks and Haki Madhubuti.

Byron was not your uncle by blood. He was an uncle by feel, also a migrant to Philadelphia. One of the few Black men who taught at the school you attended back then. He lived across the street from the school with his family, and the home held African art, and they played beats and loved each other and laughed over blood-warming drinks.

At school one day, Freeman, a teacher announced Byron's death. I'm sure you remember. You burst into tears. They called me, guiltily, not having imagined that since you hadn't had him as a teacher and weren't a member of his family, that it would affect you so badly. He wasn't an uncle by blood or marriage, but by love. He was my friend. It hadn't occurred to them that a deeper connection might be present anywhere, that someone in the group of middle schoolers might weep for the Black male school leader who had made space for them. That kinship happened in other ways than the ways that were common to them.

A few weeks earlier, Issa, you had seen your Uncle Byron in his yard while your class was on a walk. You waved and said, "Hey, Uncle Byron." You recalled later that he seemed frail, but he smiled at you warmly and said, "Hey, Is." One of the other children said, "That's not your uncle." You insisted. Of course he was.

This is our culture. It is a beautiful thing, you know. Back in slavery times, when the nation and its laws said we had no right to family, to the kinship structures of blood and law, we made another set of relations, bindings, family. Family is more than that, we testified. And we kept it up, and we hold it, even when it might look like we have assimilated. Even after death.

We bind where law fails and rules miss.

You are so young and yet you have lost so many people you love. Some so early you can only remember them from the times I have repeated their stories, the moments they shared with you. I have given you the taste of re-memory, its sweetness like a private showing of history. And you have learned of so many dead children. I have worried about it. But I can't change it. I can't hide the disappearances. I can't pretend your tears shouldn't be flowing. They should. And you will learn not only to grieve but also to chat with death. Because running from it will haunt you in irreparable ways. Instead you must turn over this reality in your hands, mix it into the clay of your living. Live in the labyrinth instead of trying to escape its fortress. Byron's story taught me the doubleness of the phrase "shooting the gift." In hip-hop, shooting the gift means to let forth the brilliance, to exercise it fully no matter what. And the urgency of that call, I happen to think, has something to do with how much our gifts are shot down. Death creeps along the edges of the costs of being Black. Hypervigilant panic is our misfortune, so much so, in my case, that the system for my body's protection has turned on me. It reaches beyond gun violence. To the lupus I have. To the sarcoidosis and congestive heart failure Byron had. And even when the body doesn't go awry, the hurt can make you trip over yourself, chasing a sweet spot to avoid feeling the pain up close. Moments of grace that can kill you. No, you just have to learn to live with the ache.

One morning we drove down Chew Avenue. It was in the 7 a.m. hour. A kitten lay dead on its side, tiny and bloodless. How did it die? Was it taken down in a street fight? Was it an unwanted runt? Had it eaten peanut-butter-tasting poison intended for rats? Had it been hit, and though able to leap enough not to be crushed, hit hard enough to make an arc just a taste off the ground, and left on its side? Orange and small. That's sad, you said. It reminded me of the day you stopped eating chicken, Issa. You looked at me, furiously and teary, and said, "I can't eat them. They just kill chickens. They just kill them, and they're defenseless, like Black people." I felt the world on your chest. You were eleven.

———

Golden's skin was like wet sand dried into dust and his hair, copper knots. He was so slim and soft but raspy voiced, back straight like a ramrod. Everything hung off him, looked like it was handed down already worn out. His shoes gaped around his ankles. He was a "Cabrini Kid" and pretty as an angel. What I remember most about Golden is him walking alone. He must have played; we all did. But he cast a solitary shadow, as though he were at work when all of us were in the glorified daycare called, humorously, camp, in a basement on the West Side of Chicago.

In Chicago, at New City YMCA, I was a visitor, and yet I blended so smoothly, visually at least. I have always, when in Black spaces, become physically indistinguishable. In the US, in Jamaica, in the Dominican Republic, in Brixton. I am Black and local. One day I was at the Jewel grocery store near Uptown in Chicago and some boys ran up behind me, "Tamika, where you get a dollar?!" They had mistaken me for their sister. I was wearing my hair in single plaits, a yellow overall short set, Keds, and a red raincoat. When they realized I wasn't her, they just wandered away. No words of confusion. I just as well might have been her. This is why when Lil Wayne said, "You don't see me on the block, I ain't trying to hide, I blend in with the hood, I'm camouflage," it feels like a personal testimony for me. Your mother is "matter of fact" Black.

I am indistinguishable differently in white spaces. Not because I blend in easily and "look like I'm from there" but because I'm faceless. I hate to say that you've experienced facelessness too. And you probably will again. You have been called the names of a plethora of different Black people. Sometimes by people who you see every day. The very thing that makes me feel so happy and comfortable wherever many Black people reside, I think, is the thing that makes me faceless where so many white people do.

When Wole Soyinka came to Princeton to give lectures, he said to me, "I know you!" And he did. We had met some twenty years earlier at Harvard. And I nearly cried from the honor of being seen. That his eyes had the capacity to remember my face was a reminder that I am not in fact an invisible woman. I did not know how to express my gratitude. But it was great. And maybe the recognition was meaningful to him too.

It was the same day that Soyinka, speaking of the girls stolen from their schools by Boko Haram, said one of them might be the next Mae Jemison. Yes, a black girl, nothing more and nothing else, from Nigeria might become, in the way a black girl from Alabama had become, someone who traveled amongst the stars. A long distant common genealogy, a sameness of form, a meaning beyond the lexicon of the world, girls with the second sight to cipher a heretofore unseen possibility.

During Chicago summers I braided the other girls' hair in the mornings because I was good at it and it helped their mothers. I could cornrow and do plaits. Hair that was heavy silky and waved, hair that was cottony and coily, abundant and sparse. I knew how to be gentle with the tender-headed girls and make the surface of the hair glow with the sheen of well-brushed, coarse thick hair. The Christie beauty shop doll head that my mother had bought me served me well. To fit was to be trusted. We dressed the same. I wasn't the only one with a white daddy who was not my biological father. Quilted bindings were ordinary. There were other bookworms too. But the truth was, I was never a constant West Side kid. I moved around and through and in and out of Black America as a child. I know what I'm talking about. I had too much sense to hate dandelions or to honor the border patrol of gardens. I picked and delighted in the beauty of cultivated gardens and weeds both. We were all both: Golden was golden; I was the color of red dirt.

I watched Golden, curiously. Every once in a while he laughed a big laugh, and his mouth would freeze, wide open and smiling. He arched back, or forward, still statuesque.

But those moments were unusual. I think I took a liking to him mostly because we shared a trait. Just like people would say, "Imani don't mess with nobody," they would say the same of Golden. He minded his business.

If Black Chicago sounds like one song it is the live recording of Lou Rawls singing "Tobacco Road." Country, bittersweet, and gutbucket but street-smart and savvy. But when I was a little girl there, what we listened to was house music. It was the latest blend of industry and religious intercession. Electronic, driving beats, a high-hat, the sounds of cymbals that made you want to jump higher and higher still.

As a retreat, I suppose, the YMCA sent us, a passel of Black children of the West Side, to the country each August, right before school was going to start back up. But a week in rural Illinois for ghetto children was lost on me. Maybe because I was born in Alabama and went home often, trees held no novelty for me. The wooded routes of bucks and birds were to be avoided, of course, but I knew what it meant for them to be just outside my line of sight.

The camp's communal showers horrified me. I have had a prissy modesty as far back as I can remember. The sound of Midwestern crickets made me itch. There were no beautiful lightning bugs. The institutional food was nasty. But I went, twice. It happened the first time, I think. Back then, adults seemed to always turn away no matter what ugly things boys did. The white boys at my school shoved their hands up girls' shirts in games of tackle and I watched from the sidelines. Here, in Chicago, I was in the thrall but still spared traumatic gender play games. This time some boys had—and this is what I had heard which was likely third-hand by then—taken Kristina, Golden's little sister, into their cabin and stripped her. She scrambled and got her clothes on. I remember her running out, scowling in a way that was more heart-wrenching than any tears. And I remember the adults did nothing.

Cabrini Green, an infamous sky-scraping housing project, Golden and Kristina's home, was a sparse enclosure. A recipe for claustrophobia and acrophobia, dim, crowded and vacant yet teeming. But the woods were unbounded. And maybe that was why the commonsensical cardinal rule was breached. "Don't mess with kids from Cabrini." Those boys had messed with kids from Cabrini.

Golden was silent. I think he wore a gray tank top. He stormed into the woods and came out with a massive branch. The offenders saw him coming. They were bigger and more numerous than Golden, but they didn't stand to defend their assault. They ran and locked themselves in their cabin.

Golden stood outside that cabin. He held the branch up high. Poised and angry. He stayed there. Hour after hour. The adults ushered us to the pool and to dinner. They were close-mouthed and pretended they couldn't see what we were witnessing. He stood there. The offending boys cowered behind the cabin door. I saw water in Golden's eyes. His back tensed, his legs apart like he was straddling a bull. Night fell and still he stood. I could see his shadowy form outside the window above Tashunda's bunk. Tashunda said, "Mmm," and I sighed. Black children are the best at banter and gossip. Guffaws, playacting, and flourish make for good fun. But there was none of that that night, just a little speculation about how bad those boys were gonna get their asses beat.

I woke up at dawn and looked out. Golden was still there. I climbed back into my bunk and drifted off again. By the real morning he was gone from his post. I don't know what happened. I imagine that finally one of the grown men had brokered some kind of peace. The rest of the week, the offending boys walked around contrite. Golden hovered around his sister. He was eleven.

I heard enough sad stories for two lifetimes those summers. Things that I should have told to an adult, but adults had proven to be unreliable at nursing wounds, at even admitting we were surrounded by them and bleeding. And we, especially us girls, would instead consult each other about how to manage pain. But there was something about Golden and the thick stillness of him holding that stick that became part of me growing up. The public-health posters, black and gray with white letters, said lead paint and leaded gas were a minefield of brain stilling. People also said the violence was caused by lead paint. I understood that the violence was caused by the layers of anguish piled up. The lead paint was a consequence, not a cause, of people being discarded.

I felt like I understood Golden, but maybe I didn't. What I saw was something that I do know to be true. Feeling deep love and complete helplessness to protect the beloveds is a fact of Black life. No matter what, he could not erase his sister's trauma. He stood outside it, raging and loving. And the night after we girls had surrounded her with affection, she smoothed her surface. I understood that too. She protected him as well as herself.

I didn't choose to change Golden's name on these pages. I don't know what happened to Golden. I looked and looked. Had he become a doctor or a teacher? Maybe a businessman. Or was he locked up or dead? Any of those is possible. There are so many Black men and women named Golden. I can't find him.

I want to leave his name intact so that if I am wrong about him and what he did and who he was, if I remember wrong, he can show up and tell me where I failed. He matters so much in my memory, I at least owe him that.

It wasn't all heartbreak. Other moments were light-hearted. We sang "Ding Dong" on every bus ride we took those summers. The refrain of the song is "Yo mama don't wear no drawers" and is part of a series of rhyming couplets shouted in a jubilant call and response. Years later I found the song in a book Richard Wright published in 1938 and figured it had traveled up to Chicago from his home in Mississippi. An inheritance. We also sang a silly riff on "Children Go Where I Send Thee" called "Going Out with Cindy." The laughter was the warmest I've ever known.

Out there in the country that week, we tried archery and I literally couldn't get the arrow out of the bow. Known for my muscled arms, I found they were clearly more show than substance. We rowed unstable boats. We danced hard to house music in the cafeteria and swung flashlights around to feel like we were surrounded by strobe lights. A makeshift nightclub, and we jumped to the high-hat, and spun around, and "worked to the bone" all the way down to the floor, sweaty and exhilarated. In our cabin, the one for the big girls, Tashunda told Jason stories at night. Most of them ended with somebody in the cabin getting killed, often in a boat on Crystal Lake. Sometimes she told the stories during the day too. Once, we were walking to the cafeteria, and she looked at me with her wide eyes and said, "Jason hit my mama over the head with a two by four and her head rolled down that very hill!" and pointed to a small, nondescript mound. I cackled.

Tashunda's nickname was Dizzy, because a counselor said she was a "dizzy broad." I knew it was cruel but I didn't say anything. Tashunda was a brilliant storyteller with perfect comic timing. Her plaits were done without clamps or elastic bands, and she dressed like a Pentecostal girl in skirts past her knees and high knee socks. She often rolled her eyes with a halfway absent posture, and the whites showed all around. Out of the basic stuff—hardware and horror films—she made us laugh. One night though, somebody else told a Jason story. And they made it about her. At the end, the girl announced that Dizzy was dead. Everyone laughed. Tashunda cried. She cried long and inconsolably. And I was too scared to consider what had really happened to cause those many tears.

It is not so uncommon today for children to move around the country. But when I was young, it was unusual. It made me at once unsettled and familiar with so much. Alabama was home; Cambridge, Massachusetts, was where I went to school; Chicago was where I spent most of my summers and holidays, except for the time I spent at home. And then in the midst of that there was Milwaukee too. And precious visits to Los Angeles with my auntie.

When my mother and I moved to Massachusetts, we moved into Harvard graduate student housing, and the variety of people made me ask her if we were still in America. The playground looked like the children's books I had depicting people from every nation. My first friend was Jaysumma. We found each other because I was wandering and not looking where I was going. He was riding a horse swing. It was metal, white and low slung. He swung. I walked.

We crashed. I crumpled on the ground. I cried. He cried. And then he thought to take me to his house. I was five. He was six.

He lived directly out of the gate and across the street. Up three steps. Inside, as I would later learn, it was always shadowy and filled with the smell of warm dye. Ashley, his mother, was a patrician turned batik artist. She wore her long, thick, straw-colored hair functionally, in a French braid down her back. When I was hurt, that day and other days, she tilted my head to the side and examined with great concern. Proposed how we might take care of it: Ice? A compress? Later, she would have me sit on the chaise longue outside her room and I would fall asleep.

That day, right after the fortuitous collision, my mother came by, and the two mothers, Theresa and Ashley, made friends.

I loved Jaysumma with abandon. His voice was raspy and tough. He was, as my grandmother would say, "all boy." He liked dirt bikes and corduroys and wore sneakers that were worn to almost nothing. And he was pretty. All lashes and jet black hair, muscled and wiry. A Black boy who could have easily blended in in Bangladesh. He was, with some irony, also delicate.

I was hardy. Small and skinny, but solidly made. My smile was big, my wispy hair escaped every clamp. Brown like a million and one other brown girls, and capable too. Soon after we made friends, my job, and Ashley taught me to do it well, was to check on Jaysumma while we played. She instructed me one day while we stood in front of the dining table. She told me to put my ear to his chest. He giggled, embarrassed. I did it. "Can you hear the whistling sound?" she asked.

Yes, I heard it. It was like a tea kettle not quite boiling. "When you hear that, bring him home. He has to stop playing and take medicine."

I suppose the expectation that I would care for my friend, when I was a year younger and a head shorter than he was, had something to do with my being a girl. But it came to me naturally. I had a room full of baby dolls, and I cooed over real babies whenever I could. I liked old people, too, to bring them things like a glass of water or their glasses. I wanted to be a mama and a helper. But it never felt like a burden to be charged with looking after another. Maybe because I didn't have to do it all the time. Maybe because I had plenty of hours to spend sitting next to the radiator with a book resting on my knees. Maybe because I knew it meant that adults found me reliable and responsible and I was proud of that. Also certainly because I am a born mama, a nurturer by disposition. You two are as well. I take that as some of your freedom. You haven't been dragged out of it by the burdens placed on boys. You know how to tend and settle and play with little people. You have the touch of care too. I hope that is something I have passed on to you by example.

It was a challenge. Jaysumma would be outside doing his boy bravado, fast and sometimes in the middle of confrontation. And I would pull his arm and hold him still and listen. It was not a task I could undertake lightly. I had to tune out every other sound and close my eyes against the sun. Is he making it? I would ask myself. I did not know then how vulnerable he felt. I only knew how vulnerable he was, and that I could be the person to keep him alive.

Labored breathing, but yes he was breathing still.

Fly

Our history is the stuff rhumbas are made of,
mambos, the jitterbug. . . . All of which goes to show
that our people could fly as the saying declares.

—NTOZAKE SHANGE[1]

My favorite Gwendolyn Brooks poem is called "The Life of Lincoln West." Lincoln is a little boy, very black in the Negroid sense, and therefore very ugly to many. He is at the movies with his mother, and a white man, with anthropological zeal, asserts that his ugliness is representative, that he is "the real thing." For Lincoln, the mark of authenticity, to be the real thing, can be turned over in his head. He is something, reviled yet real.

When the world is bent on you not becoming, being and becoming is an uphill battle that can become Sisyphean. You just keep rolling down that hill. Not because we cannot love ourselves or find ourselves. We can. It is that every step towards that becoming gets classified. "Good Negroes" are obedient to the rules of white supremacy in one way or another. The bad ones merit destruction. You can be both in one body, depending on the day. The smallest of gestures or infractions can be spiraled into trenchant myth.

Old-fashioned lore about Black people talked about what was under folks' clothes. They claimed we had tails. The human vestigiality, that is, the coccyx bone, is a reminder of before we were who we are, an overgrowth that rests behind us, hidden by our modesty. There is a remnant there, but the tale was a lie.

Doctors also used to say African scapulas were abnormally wide. I prefer that lie, or to turn it into a way of telling a truth. Broad like a monarch butterfly's wings on that expanse we learn to hold in a state of grace. The training begins early. My mother used to say, "Stand up straight, put your shoulders back." And I said it to you. No stooping, no obeisance. That is your body's testimony.

How do you become in a world bent on you not being and not becoming? After the war for emancipation, after almost a decade of freedom, the door slammed shut. Young men, who thought standing was a part of freedom, stood in front of corner stores. They might have been telling big lies, or chewing on some tobacco, or talking getting out of this town. And a white man driving a horse-drawn buggy would come and catch them up. How many generations before this was done? Vagrancy. That was the easiest cause of action against young men standing on the corner.

What could happen then? The state could sell you to the highest bidder. And off in the swamps your freedom meant nothing. You were chained together. Worked near to death. Stalked with ugly eyes.

The watchmen remain.

Today, young Black people are probed and searched and arrested. For this, officers are compensated with promotion and raises. This means that hunting Black people is an expected part of the work of law. Inside prison the regulation of every bit of movement is an act of thieving. There is no retreat, only exclusion, isolation, and enclosure. They shatter life inside. They grind the tiniest of shards into the dirt. So much theft of what is. So much of becoming is siphoned away. George Bernard Shaw said if you want to understand a society, look at its prisons. Our prisons are Black. Like you. Like me.

Eyes watch you. The world is filled with watchmen, poised for your error meriting correction or punishment. Muscles threaten to tighten in response. To not unfurl or stretch. To not grow. But even if you are under their gaze, being and becoming require you to be much more than what is under their gaze, to unfurl and expand under adverse circumstances. That is yeoman's labor. Everywhere you go, captivity haunts. You know they are there even when they are not. Emily Dickinson was right. Haunting doesn't require a physical location. The brain is much vaster than any property and place. A terrifying specter is haunting our

Blackness: the white imagination. A magnificent specter haunts our spirits, the persistent selfness that refuses the undifferentiated fictional mass of Blackness. Each one of us is marvelously particular. That is what being human, in large part, means. And yet each of us finds ourself at least in part through the eyes of another. What a complicated dynamic. And then there is the general beast of American culture. Americanness has a perverse imperative. To be all the same and to be distinguished in order to be of value. And to be distinguished, according to the American beast, is to always be quantifiable and superlative: the best, the most. For the dark amongst us, it is different. One must be distinguished doubly, from the masses and from Blackness, and yet always with the conscious awareness of being inferior and subject to the larger white world's constant evaluation as to whether or not you are worthy.

Freeman, you arrived an independent fugitive. You began to use me as a ladder when your thighs were still new-baby skinny. You stabilized yourself in tiny pale bootie-covered feet and positioned yourself at an angle across me. And then the older you got, the higher you climbed, always reaching over my shoulder.

I remember. You were two years old and you insisted upon a puzzle that sat atop the mantel. I said no. Someone, who irritated me with the gesture, had given you a seventy-piece puzzle. Too much for a baby. I anticipated a meltdown of frustration. I was tired myself. I said no, and because you were even then well-behaved, you changed your attention to some toys on the floor. I went into the kitchen to make you some lunch.

When I returned, you smiled triumphantly. There was the puzzle. On the floor. Completed.

There was something mystical about you. You did downward-facing dog when you were a toddler, as though you were a yogi in a past life. You waved at your grandfather in the hallway after he died, saying, "Hi, Pop Pop!" And you had a recurring nightmare about the Guédé. You called them "Getty Guardians." The Haitian Loas, short, hatted, and fast, chased you in your dreams like the Klan chased me in mine when I was a child. My blood turned cold the first time you talked about them. I settled, however, remembering that dreams and nightmares are both products of a beautiful imagination. There has always been something ethereal and esoteric about your gift as an artist. You work at it, but you are also channeling, accessing something beyond what we see right here before us. It is like the science fiction novels you plot in your free time. You can see another world. This gives me hope that you might evade the tempestuous gridlock of social assignations.

Grandpa used to take me to Shakespearean comedies. It started because one day *A Midsummer Night's Dream* was playing on our television. The TV sat on a dining chair, with pliers on top of it. We used those to change the channels. A hanger replaced a broken antenna. He said I paid rapt attention to every scratchy black-and-white moment.

So we went to Shakespeare in the park. Outside on warm summer nights, Chicago went from sweltering to mild. The scent of grass and exhaust amused me. The players enchanted me. My favorite was *The Tempest*. My favorite character was Ariel. The sprite was held captive in a tree for twelve years by the sorceress Sycorax. Prospero the magician freed them (Ariel was ungendered), but then Ariel was bound in service. The promise was if Ariel were to do Prospero's full bidding, freedom would finally come. A dutiful servant with the gift of flight and language, Ariel's freedom is finally earned at the end. To me, that, more than the marriage that Ariel facilitated between Prospero's daughter and her beloved, was what made me leave the play satisfied.

When I got to college, I learned that as a Black person I probably ought to have paid greater attention to Caliban. The inhabitant of the island, the colonized one, the half-monster son of Sycorax. My professors lectured on the meaning of him stealing books that he could not yet read. Aimé Césaire made him into a revolting slave; Robert Browning made him into a theologian. He is resentful, confused, and defeated. But he is also a more complex and questioning character, not dutiful but probing.

Sometimes I think we in Black America are assigned to be one or the other. Both captives, whatever sense of freedom we might have always hinging on the grace afforded by the powerful white magicians. I say that, but I am not resigned to it. I don't want you to be either. Be not reconciled to injustice but also not devastated.

Imagine yourself instead on that island in the ways you have been at the sweetest moments of life. Tulum, Nassau, Massachusetts. Your feet of burnished bronze at the edge of the ocean. The air tastes like salt. You run into waves. The veil is rent and you move with abandon. Your whole life you have been told you cannot do this, but then sometimes you can.

Islands are surrounded by water. Water is a complex and confusing element. It soothes and heals. It gives life. And it dances furiously, wrecking and drowning. It is a graveyard, as the African bones testify from the Atlantic floor, and it can hold you aloft above its depth. Survivors will sing it. It can swing open the gates of death. When you dance at water's edge, literally but also in terms of meaning alone, it is an unbounded joy. A way of simply being. A rare and miraculous gift. All of that to say, enjoy the play but remove the bindings.

I know, those moments are temporary. Most of the time the fact of your Blackness keeps you tethered to some unpleasant things, and not just the beauty of it. It is bad enough that you have to endure. But they want you to tell it as though you are their entertainment and they are not indebted to you. People will ask you to tell the story of your suffering or exception, or both, as you navigate the world. They will not just say, You must either be Ariel or Caliban; they will ask you to perform it. I cannot tell you what to do with the fact of your suffering or your distinction. With the mis-narrated stories and the truthful ones. But I must tell you that is a trap, a caricature of your existence. It forces you into two dimensions when you are in four.

When I was a little girl, I used to listen to the same al-bums, over and over. Repeating lyrics like chanting, or an intercession, or a meditation and mediation between me and them, and where they came from and where I came from. I wept for certain songs: Al Jarreau's "Milwaukee"—because I was a perennially homesick person. And Jimmy Cliff's "Many Rivers to Cross." There is a line in that one, "Wan-dering I am lost as I travel along the White Cliffs of Dover." I have only recently begun to pay attention to it. A Jamaican man, in a Jamaican story, a child of the transatlantic slave trade and colonialism at once, sang about the geographical symbol of British empire. It has hit me, finally. Let me step back, I know, and I have told you, that we are both African and of the West, like most Africans are. Black Americans are a genealogically and culturally mixed people. We cannot aspire to purity; our new languages and new cultures are not shameful—though the histories that produced them are the shame of those who oppressed and those who reap the benefits of that oppression. But only recently have I been willing to take seriously the question of what it means to wander in the midst of this story, to name a homeplace in the middle. It is easy to critique, to deconstruct, to analyze. It is harder to find one's footing as a life journey in it. You physically stand in classrooms where you are one of a few Black children. You historically and politically sit in a landscape of white supremacist history. The decisions about what to do with that are lifelong. For some, it is a matter-of-fact reality. For others, it is a bitter pill that gets stuck in the craw. Some choose to name themselves an eternal opponent. Although your names proclaim a relation to it: Freeman, and Diallo, meaning bold one. Or Issa, meaning "salvation," and Garner, "that which is worked for," "earned." These choices are personal ones.

I am riding in a taxi in Boston. The driver asks me, "Do you know what your name means?" His name is Mohammed. I tell him my name means faith. I mention it is a name in Arabic, Hausa, and Swahili. He goes on, "In my language it is 'believer.' In Persian, Farsi, Urdu . . . maybe even Hindi." Americans, he reflects, don't often take these names. But elsewhere they do. He says, They don't have to mean religious things. They can be chosen for their beauty. Yes I know. I tell him about the names in my Catholic, Christian family: Rasheeda, Jamilah, Kamilah, Nia … He repeats them back to me with meanings I know. I say, "My son is Issa."

"Jesus."

"Yes. And 'river' in Songhai. And 'salvation.'"

History is duress. Mohammed said to me, "Your name is your character." And again, Wole Soyinka said, "The assault on human dignity is one of the prime goals of the visitation of fear, a prelude to the domination of the mind and the triumph of power." Hold your head aloft. Carry your name, free men. Yes, we are afraid, but we cannot wear terror around our necks like cowbells for our own denigration, no matter how lost we sometimes feel, no matter how dangerous the poisons. And they are plural: Boone's Farm wine and Mad Dog malt liquor, landfills and toxic waste, Flint's water, crack, and the lie that you are insufficient.

Boot was poisoned.

My eldest uncle died when he was nine years old. His skin was dark brown like his grandfather's. But Roland Larue, or "Boot" as they called him, was not like his grandfather. The Reverend L. D. Perry was a mean man who drove most of his eighteen children away from home or mad with his cruelty. But maybe he hadn't been cruel once. Maybe when he was known mostly as Leman instead of Reverend Perry, he was sweet and gentle.

My mother remembers her brother, even though he died when she was a toddler. She remembers when he was sick, and she, a three-year-old, used to climb up in the big dark-wood bed in the blue room to play with him. She remembers he was sweet and gentle and generous. And then he was gone.

Before he was sick, my grandmother walked Boot to school each day. She told me she had to, because she dressed him in a suit with short pants for school. Every day. And so in order to prevent him from being beat up, she walked him. The thought of him not wearing a suit, she recalled, laughing, did not occur to her. School was an important occasion.

What would have happened to Boot had he lived? We don't know. What kind of man would he have been? Would he have been my favorite uncle? Would he have been the first to graduate from college? Would he have been a brilliant scholar like his younger siblings? Would he have been a source of amusement for cruel white boys and robbed from us later and even more bitterly? We don't know. What if?

You know what could have happened? Boot could have lived. He could have, like Du Bois once speculated of his dead child, rent the veil of the color line in two. He could have, like the two siblings he knew when he died, lived to integrate and redistribute and champion freedom. He could have traveled far afield like to Los Angeles and Boston, like his baby sisters, long after his death. He could have led a movement. Or maybe he would have continued impaired, from the ongoing impact of the strong medicine or the stronger disease. He might have been an invalid genius who never left the back room except in his vast imagination. What if he was too afraid, after having felt the pressure of shallow lungs, of pushing too hard, of hoping too much? What if he had been the one, the only one, who couldn't achieve against the odds?

What if he had soared?

Do angels have wings? How many of them can dance on the head of a pin? The answer: infinite. They aren't bound to space or reality. Boot crossed over. You carry his wings. I will not speculate about reincarnation, visitation, or the prospect of sharing past and future lives with other souls. All I know is that the tribe increases no matter what. And the future is unknown.

You are both older than he ever lived to be. He is still nine. Before you know it, you will be grown men. But for now, you are in the first and most stormy stage of growing up. I happen to believe we never stop growing up, and that is my secret for not feeling regret. My failures are my lessons, but I can always get better.

But this stormy stage of growing up is not like any other because it is your first, and maybe even your only, conversion experience. Such becoming is indecorous. It is often unbecoming. "Becoming" is a funny word, because it means beautiful as well as the process of arriving at a state of being. I like that. It is ironic and also ambiguous. Such becoming isn't a mere look; it is a doing. You are both conventionally beautiful in your exterior and also conventionally demonized in your exterior. Black and beautiful. Loud and very quiet, laughing and scowling and sometimes irreverent and sometimes way too observant to feel peace. You are doing this living thing and growing thing, and it is tough and that is beautiful. It is also ugly. There is a concept: ugly-beautiful; *jolie laide* is the French expression used to describe someone who is unconventionally beautiful. Like someone with buck teeth whom we think is cute. Or someone who has a personality so captivating that one look at the person makes our heart flutter. That's it, but in a different way.

From the time you were little, I have made up absurd stories. Some of them involve the personage Mephistopheles. He is a bumbling character whose name is pronounced as though he were a wacky cartoon sea lion wearing a bowtie. You outwit his antics, and they are goofy. Things like trying to ski on the top of a skyscraper or eat all the plums in the world. In these stories, he isn't evil, like in the Faustian ones, although he is unwittingly snared into things that don't make sense by his own misperceptions. It is funny, but it is also a warning. Things that are completely absurd, that make you laugh, can on a dime turn to harrowing. At one of my high schools the one rule, they used to say, was don't roller-skate in the hallways, which basically meant "Don't be a jackass." Don't be a jackass. Of course, we sometimes are. But we have to try to minimize it all. Because as human as we are, something divine is required for us to make it over.

Our wings get tattered. We sometimes thrash. Or bruise. Purple marks that remind us of our aching hearts. We are treated in ugly ways; they penetrate and shape us, but the struggle is more than beautiful. The fight in the face of it makes a *jolie laide* life. Reckonings are our lifestyle. What to make of this juxtaposition, this double consciousness, this doing and being and feeling and, yes, becoming.

The two of you remind me of my values. For instance, there was the time, Freeman, that I suggested you change your outfit for the antiviolence protest downtown. I wanted you to put on something a bit sharper. You reminded me that looking cute wasn't the point. Sometimes when I impose my rules of decorum and presentation, Southern working-class rules, you remind me that I can put too much emphasis on appearance. That might be true. But I believe that some of these ways of doing and being matter only because they are an example of self-regard, a claim of your own value, no matter what the national messages have been about our undeservedness and inadequacy.

You agree. I know you do. You each take pleasure in your self-fashioning. You like being fly. Brilliant hoodies and distinctive sneakers. Hair that is at once styled and wild. You appraise yourself in the mirror with appreciation. I love that. It is like that—knowing what feels good, what matters, what really matters, what sometimes matters—is what helps you make it through, what reminds you who you are.

We were on the Peter Pan bus this time, going up to Woods Hole, on the coast of Cape Cod. I don't know why. Maybe cars were in the shop, maybe the cash was low. This was before you were born. This was when I went everywhere I could with my friends. This was when you could get a car onto the island ferry going standby. When Martha's Vineyard was a New England thing and a Black thing but not publicly a presidential super-elite thing. Omar was entertaining the bus with jokes. One was about his cousin Naomi. "We woulda been there by now if Naomi was driving. Naomi be flying." It was repeated at least four times: "Word. Naomi be flying." "True, Naomi be flying." Smiles and shaking heads.

Driving fast. Like you can outpace every burden, every weight upon your shoulders, every fear and every danger. It is exhilarating when you are young. And terribly dangerous.

A reckless sense of freedom, a sign of failed judgment and a yearning. Let me be supremely reckless. I am your mother and so I never want you to be reckless at all. And yet, I know that thrill. I remember it as part of the sweetness of youth. I would prefer you satisfy it not with fast cars or hard drinking, but with laughing and dancing all night and over-sleeping and taking unexpected road trips to places where you discover things, inside yourself, that you hadn't even speculated.

I want to hold you safe. I also want you to fly.

The routes have always been rough. West Africa to Barba-dos to South Carolina. Maryland to Alabama. To Chicago from Mississippi. By boat, by train, by foot, each time an unsteady cruelty. You, revenant, must learn to possess an impeccable balance. Claim your earth as you see fit and ride above it.

Yes, I am asking you to do something difficult. To make beauty and love in a genocidal time, with a harrowing past behind you. But when was it easier? I have some tips on how to do it. Never let shame eat you up. Don't resolve it the American manhood way, with violence and insult as de-flection. I tell you this knowing that throughout your life, this will make you a target. Betraying the rules often does. Men who don't mistreat are always at greater risk of being mistreated. The spirit of wounded boys is a haint. The worst possible thing that rots and turns invisible. Beware of the strategic decanter; make pain a way to tell part of your story. Such grace will make you a full-hearted person. When you are hurt, cry. When you are humiliated, let the sadness be at least as present as the rage. Make the moments of its release be under the arm of protection, a moveable feast. The lord says vengeance is mine. Give it up to God.

You do not do any of this alone. Even in the most private recesses, you carry a history with you. Like the phoenix, in you the ancestors come again, rise from the curling red and gray ashes underneath lynching trees. You return after so much combustion and hunger. Sempiternal and everlasting. That is what Black reincarnation is. The debt is still owed. We keep making generations to collect our inheritance.

There isn't much agreement about what that inheritance is though. I will admit that to you. We are American, profoundly so. Its scullery maids and its children. Offspring of this beautiful ugly nation.

In Sylvia Plath's striking poem "Ariel," she writes of "nigger-eye berries."[2] Coming across it is one of those offputting events, like being ten and seeing *Ten Little Niggers* in the card catalog when looking for a new book from one of my favorite mystery writers, Agatha Christie. Disappointing and yet so unsurprising. The last line of Plath's poem is "Eye, the cauldron of morning." It makes me think of America, always cooking up death with the new day only possible in the mind's eye, in the wake of mourning, with the imagination. The eye of the nigger is a metaphor, I am convinced. Unintentional perhaps, but profound. Our gaze is the sharpest yet.

"Nigger-eye berries" mean blackberries. If you bite into one, the ink dashes through the pale juice. There is black sight. There it is swallowed up. There is the distasteful metaphor. There is the truth.

Freeman, you are intolerant of the patience we are told to have with racism in literature. You hated *To Kill a Mockingbird* when you first read it. At first, I was irritated with you. Just read this classic, don't be precious, I thought. But then I saw that you were right, at least about what we have all made of the book. Atticus is not a hero; he is a two-dimensional caricature of one, and unrealistic at that. And Tom is merely a noble savage. He has no insides; he is not brilliantly drawn. I betrayed what I had taught you when I expected you to be sympathetic to beloved characters who hate or mock you. I should have known better.

Your lesson to me is the consequence of my own education. I have taught you to not love white people. That sentence may get me in trouble. Of course, you love individual white people. I do too. Many in fact. But I have taught you to not love them as a group. Because whiteness as such means hating oneself. And I have taught you to love Black people. Of course, there are individual Black people that you dislike or even despise. I do too. There are Black people I dislike so much I don't want to lay eyes on them. But loving Black people is not about each individual; it is about something bigger than that. Yusef Komunyakaa has a poem called "Blackberries." In the middle it goes like this:

Although I could smell old lime-covered
History, at ten I'd still hold out my hands
& berries fell into them. Eating from one
& filling a half gallon with the other,
I ate the mythology & dreamt
Of pies & cobbler [3]

We hold open our hands for certain histories; we do make choices about what we will swallow, and dream.

Blackberries are one of those things I fed you, thinking that I was being a superior mother. I also made fresh baby food with a puree machine and avoided all unnecessary sugar. For a little while. Blackberries were unfamiliar to me until adulthood. When I started to eat them, I thought they were kind of fancy. I would place them in a bowl, a pale one, to contrast against their rich color. Early, I noticed that whenever the baby ate them, a thin angry rash grew. I took you to an allergist and she said you absolutely were not allergic to blackberries. But those rashes were uncomfortable. And persistent. And definitely directly correlated to the times when you ate a big bowl of blackberries. So, I kept them from you.

Sons—

You have been running away from lies since you were born. But the truth is we do not simply run away from something; we run to something. I do not think you fully believe me, but I am not a mother who yearns for you to be a president or captain of industry. I will not brag about your famous friends or fancy cars, and I will not hang my head in shame if you possess neither. I am practical, to a certain extent. I want you to be able to eat, to keep a roof over your head, to have some leisure time, to not struggle to survive. I want you to be appreciated for your labors and gifts. But what I hope for you is nothing as small as prestige. I hope for a living passion, profound human intimacy and connection, beauty and excellence. The greatness that you achieve, the hope I have for it, for you, is a historic sort, not measured in prominence.

It is a kind rooted in the imagination. Imagination has always been our gift. That is what makes formulations like "Black people are naturally good at dancing" so offensive. Years of discipline that turn into improvisation, a mastery of grammar and an idea that turns into a movement that hadn't been precisely like that before—that is imagination, not instinct. Imagination doesn't erase nightmares, but it can repurpose them with an elaborate sense-making or trouble-making. This is what I take to be the point of the idea in Toni Morrison's *Song of Solomon*: "Wanna fly, you got to give up the shit that weighs you down." Flight is a way of transcending the material given in favor of the heretofore unseen.

Here is a confession: Recently, I have wondered if white people are irredeemable. Again, I have to issue a caveat for the sensitive. No, I do not mean individuals. Individuals are the precious bulwark against total desperation—in them we find the persistence of possibility. Of course a single person can be someone's hell. But a single person can be a heaven too. Or a friend.

But I worry that white people are irredeemable, and it scares me. What would the complete dissembling of the kingdom of identity look like? How would the viscera pulse under a cracked open surface? Would we all shatter? Could we put something together again? I don't know. I am losing some of my ability to dream a world.

Freeman, for years you have plotted elaborate science fiction novels. And you used to imagine the artificial limbs you would make one day as a prosthetics designer. You were hoping to make ones in which the flesh would respond to heat and touch. And when you were very little you loved masks: green monsters, ghosts. Issa, you preferred costumes that left your face free. In either instance, you were boys who loved to play with full flights of fancy. These were not coercive masks. They weren't the masks Paul Laurence Dunbar once described, a pleased surface presented to white America, hiding the inner roiling and rage, a survival technique. Not that. But play is complicated. The proscenium is a place of both the real and possible. The circumstance and dreaming beyond it. And the backstage is always present, parts of the interior that do not fully emerge. I want to remind you that even though you were born into a display generation, and your imagination rivets, the backstage cannot ever be forgotten.

Mothers ride the backstage of their lives frequently. Even mothers like me, who live a substantial portion of their lives center stage. I remember one day, doing an internet quiz, designed to ask your small child questions. The result was supposed to be hilarity at what the kids get wrong, like your age, and all of their frankness about things like snoring and food indulgences. I asked you, "What is something I like to do?"

You sat and contemplated. I could see you going through the inventory of details: my job, name, age, and and and. But you had no answer and were silent. I was gutted.

Anyway. Here it is: I love drinking limeade and being outside in summertime. Reading, of course, and people watching. Black-and-white movies and independent cinema. Laughter and impressions. Silliness. Beautiful fabrics. Painters who verge on the gothic. Pizzeria Regina pizza, which I haven't eaten in decades. Rain. A delicious hot bath, a long sleep. Connectedness, intimacy, semiprecious stones, being with my people—in the general and specific—and sitting in solitude. Especially while crocheting.

When I was a little girl, my windows were covered by curtains your grandmother sewed. Chinese dragon kites hung from the ceiling; a Puerto Rican flag someone gifted me and a rope of copper bells were affixed to my bedpost. I sat on the floor, by the window and the radiator to read. And dolls, my favorite kind of toy, were everywhere. In my sweet refuge of a room, I journeyed everywhere on pages and played at being a mama one day.

I used to say that one thing I would never make my children suffer from is my resentment, neither guilt nor the pain of a parent who blames you for what they fail to have. So, I wouldn't cut myself off for them, I declared as a young woman. I would model living in my own purpose and joy. Clearly I failed. I will keep trying to do better. Giving you the space to know me, gives you space to become you. At least I hope so. So, indulge me a bit more:

Everyone's story has a plethora of plotlines.

I will tell you some. You will discern some that are hidden, even from myself. Others you will hear and perhaps heed. Gabriel García Márquez said we all have a public life, a private life, and a secret life. Of the third, he said, even God doesn't know about that one.

My story, as I tell it, never stays in one lane.

I was born a regular Black girl. Brown, Alabaman. Narrow, with bowed legs and pigeon toes. The doctors corrected these features, one of which was still a mark of sexiness by the time I hit adolescence, with plaster casts. I wonder, did they actually break my legs, or control their growth? I don't know.

I was born to an unexceptional exceptional working-class Black family, known for being smart and hard-headed. You can't tell them nothing. Lots of valedictorians, lots of tales of outspokenness. Humor and composure at once.

I was born of a graduate of Exeter and Harvard, the son of a prizefighter and cook, and a Louisianan, raised in upstate New York. One of the remarkable ones, plucked from the darker ranks because of how much he sparkled.

He and my mother separated before I was born. I was raised by a Jewish communist father. A working-class kid from Brooklyn who hated school and somehow (and here

I mean somehow in terms of the labor movement and welfare-state values) ended up not where he began his working life, pushing bolts of fabric in the Garment District, but at City College, and then the University of Pittsburgh, and then Yale, and then Alabama, and then as a revolutionary.

I promise you, I am talking about myself when I say all of these things. The story I tell about myself is my constant companion. The first time I read Marita Bonner's essay "On Being Young—a Woman—and Colored," sometime in high school, I learned that what James Baldwin said was true: reading will remind you that you are not alone, even when you are lonely. Bonner wrote: "Strange longing seizes hold of you. You wish yourself back where you can lay your dollar down and sit in a dollar seat to hear voices, strings, reeds that have lifted the World out, up, beyond things that have bodies and walls."[4]

I have often wished that I was born with a caul around my face. A slippery membrane, like the flesh of a jellyfish that allows you to see ghosts. But my caul, if I could have chosen it, would walk around the history that led me to exist in this time and place. To understand myself as not only my crafted interior, but as the bloom of a certain soil.

My mother has always been the most cerebral person I know, and my grandmother was, and I know this is a cliché for Black intellectuals with working-class roots but I really do mean it, one of the most brilliant. Books were everywhere in my homes. I watched my grandmother read every day, usually the paper, with a cup of coffee, or a cut-up watermelon. I watched my mother read philosophy and sociology and ethnography. I think that is how I came to be.

My generation was oddly situated. And I was especially so. I was a child of the South, and of the movement, and of leftist intellectuals, and of the working class and of the New England educational elite. My home was always my grandmother's green kitchen and blue bedroom. The language that feels closest has always been that of the Black South. But my tongue, in most of my walk through life, is crisp. It is guarded. I keep the paths I travel at a distance. If you hear me say words like "finda," "siditty" and "sometimey," it means I trust you. You remind me of the loss when I moved up north as a little girl and became a visitor, not a resident, in my home.

The protests, the prisoners, the books: Fanon, Albert Memmi, Amilcar Cabral, Malcolm X, Karl Marx—I suppose in a sense it was a form of indoctrination. But it also convicted me. I knew, even when I looked into the pale eyes of my schoolmates, that I belonged to a bigger world of people on a mission for freedom. The books were around me; they also pulled me in. I lived in them. When my dad (who lived in Chicago) yelled at political meetings, and when my mom wrote her doctoral dissertation, my nose was in a book. Sometimes my mother left me in bookstores where I sat on the floor, for hours, reading. You have to understand: I wasn't trying to be smart. I was satisfying my yearnings. It was play and delight. It was making do. This is why I am who I am.

The teachers who saw me and cared for me were the ones who witnessed our mutual passion. The ones who believed in the magic of the human imagination and the discipline to make it art. We shared an often unspoken bond but one strong enough to keep me attached to "school" as an institution for the rest of my life. It is a place for the people who love books.

The refuge of books will never disappear. Through each heartbreak of my life, romantic and even more significantly, death, I go to pages: Reading them, writing them. It is escapism and also creativity. I have devoted my life to cultivating and curating that place inside.

This habit of retreat is shyness and sensitivity. There is a gap that usually seems difficult to traverse, even though I am fascinated by people and enjoy many of them. In college I learned that some people saw me as standoffish. And I suppose I am, but not because of a feeling of superiority but rather of incomprehensibility. I do not blame people for not understanding me. I just prefer to experience that fact in controlled doses. But here I am trying to explain myself, still.

Auntie Simone once asked me, "What are your politics?" That was many years ago. I answered, "Poor people." It was an awkward answer. But that is at the center. I think poverty is the product of an evil way of being, of hoarding and depriving. And it is a part of a web. The history of conquest is a scourge on the human condition. A lingering one. The fact of the body, the fact of who has the most weapons, the fact of which gender one finds attractive and which one to belong to, regardless of the details of the flesh, these are things I believe in making free and treating tenderly.

When I was about seven, my dad introduced me to a receptionist in his office named Jim. We walked upstairs to his office. He looked at me and asked, "Do you know what it means to be gay?" I shook my head. "Jim dates other men. Some people think that is bad. It isn't. It is unjust and oppressive for people to be mean to him because of that."

That was it. Like so many of the values of my parents that I embraced, it was easy, because they were all based in love and fairness. Two things children understand better than adults.

My mother always had, among her friends, radical Black lesbian feminists. They were women who wrote beautiful stories and made art and had the flyest apartments with nice stereo systems and delicate touches of chinoiserie. I knew, in a vague way, that people around me—whether in my neighborhood or school in Cambridge, or my neighborhood in Alabama—didn't approve of queerness. And yet I always knew there were many queer people in my midst.

I suppose this is part of what makes my upbringing unusual. I may have been taught to be ashamed of wrinkled shirts, and to believe in socialism, but I was not taught to condemn queerness, nor to champion patriarchy. Marriage was not fetishized, and I never dreamed about a wedding (although I created elaborate plans for my future prison escape after being imprisoned while fighting for the revolution and plotted where I would wash up if I ever became homeless).

If I tell this story instead: I graduated from an elite prep school, Concord Academy, then matriculated at Yale and, after completing a double major, went directly to earn a law degree and PhD from Harvard and an LLM from Georgetown, and now I have been a professor at Princeton for a decade after seven years of teaching at Rutgers Law—if I list all that, the pedigree will completely distort the listener's understanding of the tradition from whence I come. Dossiers and pedigrees can overwhelm even the most straightforward narrative, and distort me. And you.

The truth is, I am indecisive. I want to fall down deep, sparkling, and warmly dark rabbit holes of all sorts. They call this "interdisciplinarity" in my line of work. Sometimes it verges on dilettantism. But more than anything, it is passion. I live for the life of the mind and heart.

If I tell the story of my life in three poles—Alabama, the Midwest, and New England—I can give the impression of a rare Black girl, maybe even tragic, who sits at the cross-roads and never fits anywhere. That would be another easy distortion. The fact is that I don't want to fit in at all. I want to continue in the strangeness that allows me to discover myself and others.

It can be hard though. Being a Black leftist who criticizes the system (neoliberalism, the Democratic Party's somewhat seedy custodianship of Black people) gets you a fair amount of heat and anger. It would be easier to just play along. But I take the collection of values held tightly against my chest very seriously. I will not call something wrong right.

However, I'm not a purist. Obviously. I announce otherwise every day (and it really is almost every day) when I carry around my Louis Vuitton pocketbook. Judge not lest ye be judged is a reminder that this silk-slipper socialist nudges herself with while laughing. I don't have clean hands, but that fact won't keep me from telling the truth. This is not judgement, it is the practice of serving as a witness.

Reading, as you can see, is not just an avocation or a habit for me. Reading is trying to understand the world around us, with a belief that it is possible to make it sweeter and better.

My chest aches over and over again at the stagnation of selfishness, hoarding, and hostility. If you are willing to know, yours will too. I want you to. I want to teach you to witness the ugliness, to fight against it, and still to revel, delight, feel spontaneity and indulgent joy.

As my job, I teach people just a few years older than you. And one day soon (it is all going so fast) I will teach people younger than you. I stay in adolescent territory. You're traveling through it. Yet I have become a woman of a certain age, a Generation X-er, and so I rail against the habits of youngsters, even though I have chosen to be a teacher mostly because I love young people. Their discoveries are so beautiful and hilarious. They are feeling their way through. I see you both in them. I long to be for my students what I know teachers other than me will become for you. The ones who strike matches for you and teach you how to dream a world.

I want to do right by you all. Yours is a sophisticated and courageous generation—resourceful too. And yet the age you exist in is worrying. Surface is everything. It is so surface that even the most popular signifier of permanence—the tattoo—only rests on top of the flesh. The things that, in fact, can't be erased lie deeper. These things seep into the organs and muscle memory. Like the way you dance in the ocean in summertime, skin the tint of molasses taffy and redwood trees. Knocked over by waves, arms reared back, head forward, running toward them.

Your play delights. From soccer games and jerseys to *Minecraft* and *Fortnite*, trivia about animals and sports teams, drawing, making bracelets and reading and dancing and blueberry tea with lots of sugar and milk, and 365 brand golden sandwich cookies.

When I was little, my mother used to tell me "don't tarry" when we had someplace to go. Issa you do the slow roll when you are mad at me. You take your own sweet time. "Don't tarry!" But there are places for you to tarry. In Pentecostalism, tarrying is waiting for the Holy Ghost, waiting to be moved. Being tarrysome has its purposes. It is a living vibrato. Simply being and relishing. As you well know, I have not set aside childish things. We race and wrestle and giggle and tell jokes. Sounding brass and tinkling bell and driving beat: that is so much of the good in life. Relish.

I have written to you enough about freedom from the constraints. And at the same time, I worry, as I do about many in your generation of Americans, that you expect too much leisure. That the elusiveness of boredom, when entertainment is always around, makes you junkies for pleasure and relaxation. Freedom and leisure are not the same thing. Freedom is best exercised with the discipline and courage of creativity. It is commitment, not its abdication. So, I want you to have both the firm spine and the flourish, the ritual of incantation and enchantment, the wood frame and the ornamentation.

You both love music like your mama. I guess like basically everybody. So, what I am saying is in life you build the melody and harmony. That architecture is a stern discipline. And then there is time for the wail and moan, the flourish of extra notes and off-beat phrasing. Issa, remember one Halloween you dressed up as the rapper Lil Uzi Vert? He is definitely a rapper of a time past my own. He is a Philadelphian like you, but from North instead of Northwest. The year before I had helped you make a costume pun. A popular song was called "Panda," and it was rhymed by the rapper Desiigner. So you wore a panda suit, with a crown and a cape that read "Desiigner" on the back. But this time you wanted a more realistic get-up. I sprayed the twisted braids you wore then, the ones that hung in your face, with a bright-pink temporary dye. And I gave you my jewels. Crystals and rhinestones. They were wrong. They weren't nearly as ostentatious as what rappers wear, but the silhouette was right. Think about what jewels are. They are natural items, formed to look like other natural items, draped across a natural form. We cover ourselves in stars and flower petals. And sunlight. As much as we say they are simply about ostentation, they are really about exciting the imagination, playing with beauty. So even with middle-class bohemian lady jewelry on, you captured rapper chic. And your fresh Jordans and athleisure wear made the outfit even better. My jewelry came home half broken, but at the end of the night, trading candy, we were both delighted by our ingenuity.

He goes by Lil Uzi because of his delivery style. His tongue is fast. It makes sense, then, that he said that school was too slow for him. It couldn't hold his attention. Uzis, those Israeli open-bolt, blowback-operated submachine guns, came into hip-hop when they came into hoods. In the late '80s. Back when I was a teenager, one of my favorite songs was by Public Enemy "Miuzi Weighs a Ton." It was also a metaphor for shooting the gift. To dream of harnessing that power, and remaking it into the form of creative genius, I have to believe it is at heart a dream of using art to make another world.

It's also rage. When I was a teenager, hip-hop satisfied mine. My values were consistent with my Quaker education: peace, justice, nonmilitarism. But my emotions were so much more complex. Yours are, too, I believe. Before I had hip-hop to turn to, when I was a small girl, I used to close my eyes tight and after a while the blackness turned into a sparkling bevy of colors, mostly green. Eventually I would wind up at a large church, earth tones, empty, and I walked inside. Other times I would be transported to a room under the couch, outfitted with a television. An intimate loophole of retreat. As I got older, I listened with my headphones, filled with this new musical form, masterful sonic rage, and put the music up as loud as it would go. I disappeared into sound. This is living in the along. Freeman, you do that now. You go places I do not know. I get glimpses. You will tell me about a chord progression. Or a Kendrick verse. Or a fantasy land you have imagined. You are distracted in the ways I am. Satisfied by it too.

I suppose that's why I don't push too hard when I say I want you to listen to Thelonious Monk or Alice Coltrane and you resist. Monk wasn't my inspiration at fifteen or even twenty-five the way he is now. I am not one of those Black elders who wants you to listen to jazz because I believe it is superior to your music and I want you to earn your bona fides in the Black classical tradition. That intergenerational squabbling mostly bores me. I want you to listen to Monk because he is a genius teacher. You have seen demonized Black men become geniuses. Monk teaches how a Black man becomes a genius. Iconoclasm, passion, and the sternest of disciplines, the practice that refuses the lie of white supremacy.

I have over thirty versions of the standard "Body and Soul." I love Esperanza Spalding's. But most of all I love the meditations of Monk. He tries it different ways. Stomps on the key this time, graces the note that time. Permutations and modifications. He takes notes out, making pared-down chords. There is something in the deletion. As well as the practice. And the adding. Wrong and genius.

Each iteration has its own value and is also an exercise. This is only possible, this creative mastery, with the fire of experimentation, with the grounds of your dreaming broad and deliberate. Do it like Monk. The permutations he played are more than a lifetime's worth. It was, as Ralph Ellison said, a stern discipline. Ellison was talking about writing, but he was a musician first. Ellison's music teacher, Miss Harrison, told him that he must always be prepared to play his very best. This was after a concert in which he'd disappointed the music faculty. She told him, "You treated your audience as though you were some kind of confidence man with a horn. So forget it, because I will not violate my own standards by condoning sterile musicianship."[5]

She didn't say "sloppy" or "shabby." That wasn't the concern. The death knell is sterility. The form without the heart. This discipline, the one I want you to embrace, is not the sort about fitting into a particular box or a way of being or of merely being precise. It is the radical discipline of becoming.

One day I would love to play every version of "Body and Soul" that Monk recorded at once. In a cool room on a summer day, a booming orchestra with soft light and my eyes closed. Laying on crisp cotton. I would like to hear the intention in every plunk and hammer together, a symphony of times brought together. I am telling you, do it like Monk. Remember Freeman, you used to wear porkpie hats like Monk? Always traveling through history, through the archive, finding your own groove.

Play with the grammar you have been given.

I am going to talk about Bach only briefly, and probably even that will make you roll your eyes. He was an innovator in the Western musical tradition. He made music linguistic. A variety of voices and pitches, point and counterpoint, like a conversation. Bach is described as the father of the fugue. It's odd perhaps that "fugue state" in psychology is a frightening departure from one's life. And in the music, the fugue is lively.

You have heard fugues, even if you haven't listened to much Bach. Think of Nina Simone's "Love Me or Leave Me." Nina was classically trained, although her greatest heartbreak was being rejected by the classical music establishment at the Curtis Institute of Music. But her genius emerged from the shadow of that rejection. And from belonging to the Blackness that, according to her, was the cause of her rejection.

Improvisation is among the greatest gifts that Black music made to the West. It carried the fugue a step further. It displaces a staged conversation with an immediate one, requiring the musician to keep returning to his or her archive to find a way to answer. Other gifts are worried notes, shifting the pitch to transform the meaning, the embellishment of the grace note, both the modification and the excess. And of course, the incantation in moments when transcendence is necessary. Think of the ballet *The Firebird*, when the bird so bewitches the monsters with song that they are worked into an exhausting frenzy. After he is done, he can break the spell and free the captives.

Or think of the religious ecstasy the enslaved brought from across the ocean, that carried them to a place other than their captivity. Or the conjure bags, which could bend the world away from your neck.

I heard this thing recently: when dogs run into the water, goofy, stupid, and murderous, where swans are gliding, and they push and splash, a swan can defend itself by pushing the dog's head down under the water and drowning it. Now, I knew geese were aggressive. I once saw, from the height of sitting atop my father's shoulders, a pack of geese attack his ankles and calves into a pecked, swollen mess. But I had no idea about swans. Things are completely different on dry land. But in the waters, the swan has the upper hand. Imagine if a sorcerer, like the one in *Swan Lake*, turned the Blacks into the elegant white-necked creatures, leaving behind two black eyes as the only evidence of their histories. And imagine that in this story, the spell could be broken not by love but only by sinking those who unthinkingly wreaked a sloppy terror in their lives. What if?

We will never know. I'll get back to something we know better. If I ask you what is my favorite song, you will answer correctly: the Commodores' "Zoom." You've heard it more times than you can count. You see how it makes me smile and weep. You've found your own music that affects you that way. Children learn from their parents' doings. I find profound comfort in Lionel Richie's voice. He sounds like my home in Alabama. He sounds like a conjurer. But I suppose more than anything the song hopes for everything I want in the world, summed up simply in the wish that the word called freedom will someday come.

In other years, my favorite song has been one by the Staple Singers, "I'll Take You There." Mavis sings about a place free from weeping and worries, deception and suffering. She sings that she can take us all there, and I wish it were true and I love her making me believe. Sometimes in music, the truth of our soul's desire steps forward. We black folks say, when we are excited about hearing a favorite, "That is my song" or sometimes "my jam" or even "my shit." And then there are some songs that do even more to us. They catch us in the throat. To create, and to be brought to one's knees by creation. That is at the height of being human.

Sometimes you say, halfway jokingly, "Mom is a witch." Uncanny events follow me. I think you are correct, not because I have mastered the supernatural, but because I know the work of conjuring, the persistent creativity, is our antidote to the sin of our birthplace and homeland.

People say that white people did not think Black people were fully human during slavery. And sometimes they still say that today. I have never believed that was true. Having studied the law of slavery, it is very clear to me that in the antebellum period white people knew Black people were absolutely human. They were not chattel, but they were to be treated as chattel, social chimeras, fashioned by the Frankensteins of European law. To be treated as other than human when you are human is not a mistake or a flaw; it is a sin without excuse. I know that something had to be rotten in the heart of anyone who stripped and beat and raped and stole children and broke hearts with impunity and entitlement. I can see it when I encounter such evil today.

I suppose this is why I don't like the appropriation of animal language for Black living, regardless of who it's coming from. There are people who like to use the term "endangered species" to describe Black men. More often than not it comes from people who are criticizing the way the society mistreats Black people and specifically Black men. Even though I try not to pick at people's colloquialisms, I can't stomach this one. It's a bad metaphor. Black men are not a species. They, you, belong to humanity. But I suppose the symbolism is about how American selfishness sucks the life out of them, leaving them for dead in dungeons, littering their carcasses on the roads of our cities, while the newspeople say, "We have no idea what is wrong." The groups of people who are victims of this world's bloodsucking are many. Black men are not singular in that regard. But we can settle here for a moment because you belong to this category that is contemplated so infamously and has been for so long, as either predator or predated, and therefore a problem. I'll say it again: You are not a problem.

When I was little, people talked about the dodo, an extinct flightless bird. Maybe this was because of the popularity of *Alice in Wonderland*. Remember *Alice in Wonderland*? How we used to recite "The Jabberwocky" together and how I used to make you giggle at "The Walrus and the Carpenter"? Not from the movie, from our car rides and books. There's a section in the book about the Dodo's Caucus-race. It is a haphazard run around a circle in which nobody could win because there was no beginning and no end. I think the dodo was seen as funny, because of its name and its toucan nose and short legs and useless wings. The absurdity of the creature was that it was extinguished because it believed it could live peaceably with humans. Dutch sailors ate it to death. And it couldn't exactly fly away from its captors.

The dodo never seems to come up in casual conversation anymore. Unlike the flamingo and the emu, it did not have beauty to compensate for its inability to take to the air. The dodo was treated as a cruel joke. After the dodo disappeared, it continued to be mocked.

I'm glad you have wings. Mythical, symbolic, and otherwise.

The dodo got me thinking about a Rashaun Rucker drawing. It is of a mythical bird, but it is not funny. It is heart wrenching. I loved Rucker's work from the moment I first saw it because it teases like it is representational art, but it really is so deeply symbolic. And because it reminds me of your drawings, Freeman. Your preternatural ability to capture emotion and gesture with a pencil has often left me stunned. I look for where you are going in lots of artists' work, but the real magic is that we can't know.

In Rucker's work, pigeon parts come out of Black men's heads or faces . . . But this one piece especially hits me. The pigeon's wings are spread, and the man's fist is at the bottom like some even more fantastical satyr beyond the fictional language, and it is shackled by a handcuff. The wrist is a long neck. The terror of the cuff is that it might cut off the flow of blood. But it will not keep the pigeon grounded. And as long as his wings can pump, I think, even if the cuff becomes a tourniquet or a lynching rope, he will live. That pigeon is afflicted. Even if he stretches out his fingers, relaxes his fist, he still must contend with captivity.

Since you've been born, we have flown home to Birmingham at least once a year. So much so, that you identify yourself as "part Alabamian." You know the airport as the Shuttlesworth Airport. You fly into a place named for a Black man who fought against the white supremacist establishment of the city. I sometimes marvel at that. So much has changed since the time your grandmother was the ages you are now.

But do you know that air travel wasn't ever segregated? The waiting rooms were, the restrooms were, but the planes were not. I guess because it was such a luxury it wasn't necessary to separate things out to keep racism in order. But it is still something.

I always give one of you the window seat. Out in the sky, over the wing, you can see that we have departed the earth. By the time we are up, I usually stop thinking about how much has changed. Like how we used to be able to meet people at the gate. There wasn't all of that security. When it first happened, it was jarring. It was like some collective ritual of lost trust.

When I was a child, in the 1970s, before 9/11, people used to hijack planes rather than crash or bomb them. And often the hijackers were looking for a different future. Sometimes they wanted to be taken to Algeria or Cuba. They took over planes seeking revolutionary asylum and what they hoped could be utopias. Usually they failed. Sometimes Jesse Jackson would be called in to negotiate. A Black man, a political figure who moved from the movement to the halls of the establishment, he mediated between the power of the West and the rest.

Back then, if you looked up in the air and dreamed about where it might take you, you couldn't see if the plane was being hijacked. Obviously, it was too high. You would learn on the radio, or the nightly news, on one of the three stations. And up in the air you couldn't see what was happening down below, down where the Black people and the white people and everyone else was. Everything was undistinguished from above.

There is a scene in Richard Wright's novel *Native Son*, in which Bigger and his friend Gus look at a plane in the sky and Bigger asks bitterly, "Why don't they let us fly planes?"[6] That was true and also not true back then. You already know this.

You are descended from a Tuskegee family on both sides. Your great-uncle used to pour drinks for Ralph Ellison and the critic and writer Albert Murray. You know the stories of that rural oasis in the middle of the Black Belt, where the famous airmen were trained to be heroes in World War II. You know that George Washington Carver's voice was high, his genius legendary, and that he was queer, a man with a life partner with whom he spent decades deep in rural Alabama. And beloved nonetheless.

The popular stories of who Black people are, are far too simplistic. The truth is, our doctrines and refusals are elastic, whether it is homophobia, nativism, or US patriotism, the beating heart of Black life morphs through violence towards love repeatedly. We are all we got. We are of and with the least of these. And we know that.

You know that you come from a tradition of Black men who could fly and those who couldn't. People of the land and the air. The first person in my family to get some college education was my grandfather. He went to Alabama A&M. He was born on May 22 of 1914. So was the jazz musician Sun Ra, birth-named Herman "Sonny" Blount. Sonny, before he was Sun Ra, went to A&M too. And left also. They were both preternaturally gifted pianists, he and my grandfather. But my grandfather never made a career of it. He migrated to Birmingham and wrote his poems, and played his piano, and made shoes for a living. His grip on reality sometimes faltered as happens with the brilliant and suppressed. Sometimes I wish he had donned magical outfits like Sun Ra, and claimed a home in outer space, and made music all the time dressed in purple, and philosophized in the midst of the short poems he wrote, because maybe he would have lived long enough then for me to both meet him and know him. Maybe all of that imagination swirling around would have made the cancer in his lungs and the ache in his heart retreat.

But that is just a fantasy.

There are people, many of them, who assume that you have a chosen future. You are golden Black children. You have parents who went to Yale, two grandparents who went to Yale. A mother and a grandmother with doctorates from Harvard. On your father's side you will be the seventh generation college-educated. But the truth is, the greatest legacy you come from, to my mind, is of the people who found meaning beyond the doors of universities or the luster of careers. Who were themselves, even in the tiniest of ways, when there was hardly any place to be.

I cannot tell you many detailed family stories from slavery or Jim Crow, of nightmarish events or humiliations. Those were not stories to pass on, according to my grandmother, even as outspoken as she was about racism until the very end of her life. I can tell you stories of defiance. And of beauty. When my grandmother Mudeah told me stories about her childhood, white folks never appeared in them. The house did, the furniture, the baseball games, the porch swings. School days, breaking rules, labor, and love. And blueberries. I never asked what kind of blueberries were in the garden that my grandmother talked about. Maybe they were northern highbush or rabbit eye. Or the tree sparkleberry, which was a curative. Probably not though; those are bitter and tough. Or the ground blueberry that sprouts after a fire. At any rate, the flowers looked like sleeping bonnets or upside-down urns. My grandmother told me about their blueberries that were as big as grapes.

Freeman, the first to taste the world. When you were born, my grandmother met you and giggled. "'Freeman Diallo Perry Rabb'—that's a big name for a little baby!" she said. I laughed too. We had given you four last names. You carried every bit of overweighted expectation for a first-born male. I was more traditional than I knew. I was like her, an iconoclast with more than a little bit of formality in my spine.

She read books to you like she once read them to me. Sometimes I fill my purse with books, not because I am re-reading them but for comfort. Books are my familiar.

She washed your clothes every day, like she did for me. She let me cook for you, but she oversaw, making sure I didn't mess up. When you started climbing, she fussed at me, "Help him, 'Mani!" I usually refused. I hovered, but I wanted you to climb on your own. But with her, you climbed right into her lap, not over or past it. And you sat there with her. You knew a good home when you found it.

By the time you were born, Issa, Mudeah was more frag-ile. For the first time, I saw her as elderly. I took you to her. I didn't want to burden her, so I didn't put you in her arms right away. But she insisted. Give me the baby, she said, at a moment when I was at my wits' end from your whin-ing. Like before, like always, her arms released all fretful-ness and you were quiet immediately. "Get me the bottle," she told me. I did. And you, breastfed child who usually preferred my warmth to plastic, suckled the bottle settled in your great-grandmother's arms. You fell asleep. She fell asleep. You held on to each other.

When I was a little girl I asked my mother why her brother, my grandmother and grandfather's first-born, Boot, died. She said something, and what I remember is that it was because the medication they gave him was too strong. It was an adult dosage. I don't know for sure that that was true, or if that was precisely what she said in hindsight. I don't know that it was the medicine rather than the strep infection that had turned to rheumatic fever. It is not the kind of question you keep asking. You know all that had to be mustered to answer such a terrible question. So instead of seeking more detail, you hang on to what you know. I know this story about Boot. He, my mother, and my aunt Phyllis all received wooden paddles with an elastic string connecting it to a rubber ball. You were supposed to bounce the ball on the paddle. My aunt Phyllis told me that she broke hers, then took my mother's. She said, "She didn't know how to do it, so I figured I would take hers." My mother cried. And Boot, the tender big brother, gave his toy to my three-year-old mother. My aunt Phyllis said she felt terrible after that. Her brother was so good.

Do you remember Aunt Phyllis? She passed right after Mudeah. I wish you'd had more time with her. She was so much fun. She would play Taboo and Spades, and laugh and cheat. When we would go to her house in Los Angeles, she would invite the neighborhood kids over and we would all play in her pool. She cooked big trays of hot wings, and her husband, Uncle Herb, the genealogist, would show whoever would watch his old home movies and tell his long family history.

My grandmother cleaned people's homes for work before she was trained in respiratory therapy. My aunt Phyllis became the dean of the School of Nursing at UCLA. They both lived their lives in the hood. They were both brilliant. They were both regular folks. That is how we do.

But don't get me wrong. Mudeah was a striver. She sent all of those children to college by will, resourcefulness, and razor-sharp intelligence. There is a direct line from her to me to you. I do want you to honor the legacy of her labor. But I don't want you to think the ascent is the value, when the value is the person you are and can become. Regardless of circumstance.

These days, there is an older white man, I think he is Italian American, at the convenience store near my job. I notice he always says hello and good morning to customers. He often smiles and says sir. He looks at me coldly if he looks at me at all. When I say thank you, he says nothing in return. I expect it has something to do with my Blackness, although I cannot be sure. We stand across from each other at a crossroads. I have elite trappings. I am recognized for having excelled in public life. He works as a cashier. One outlet for my bitterness at his mistreatment could be to jab "How dare you think yourself superior, you work at a convenience store." But such one-upmanship, while potentially satisfying, displaces one ugly stratification for another. The Trump era has made one generalizable truth strikingly clear: a big man can be very small. A small man can be imperiously racist. To make a great deal of prominence itself is to diminish the importance of character. Don't do that. But don't be afraid to expose the shame of the racist either, with your beauty and your grace.

A few times you have been jubilant to meet famous people. I hope that you remember how we talk about the work they do, and not the fame, as what matters. I have been deliberate about having many of those people be Black men, in whom you can see an array of ways of being and pursuing passion. Rappers and ballers, writers and comedians. Writers and scholars and dancers. This is a great fortune in your eyes. Meeting heroes. I hope that the fortune it opens is not one of the wages of access, but rather the destiny that unfolds out of your life. That the encounter is one bit of your life's ignition.

I remain fearful when I hear people around us place too much emphasis on "making it." I do not want you to become addicted to that as a buffer or a bolster. Your human value is not bound to external recognition, nor is it bound to unrepentant diminishment. I do not want those to be your terms. I am voracious for juicy living for you both. You have a strong sense of it already. That you deserve belly laughs and music and color and friends. The scent of fresh rain turning dry ground moist and curiosity and passion. Time to cogitate on anything that captures your imagination. You both cry, and you're headstrong and you get angry. You have gumption, chutzpah, moxie. You know about the noble Black airmen who saved the world from Nazis, and genius Black scientists and shoemakers. You don't have to worry whether you are destined to the heights of achievement or have the ability to achieve them. You don't have to worry that your life will be empty if perchance you don't.

Your grandfather's piano sits in the front room of our family home to this day, long after its musician has passed. I tried to get you both to play. I'm fairly certain I failed at that effort because I wouldn't make you practice. You both had an inclination to the instrument, but I didn't cultivate your discipline. Sometimes, not always, the joy is fierce enough to make the discipline its own reward. I see that when you write, and take photographs, and draw . . .

The piano sits there waiting.

Upstairs, in our house, there is an electric piano. Full keys, under a black-and-white Gordon Parks photograph of two boys fishing at a creek in Alabama in 1956, and a color one of Black children, mostly girls, looking at a fair from behind a Jim Crow fence. Freeman, I sometimes catch you playing that piano. Not songs, but chords that I know you are using to figure out with some digital production.

Sometimes I am frustrated at my own failure to get you to love the piano, but most times I think that whatever you needed from it was ignited despite my failure.

In this life, I want to fill you up so much with fresh water that when you enter the deserts you have enough sustenance to endure and revel in your own possibility. So that you drink your baptismal water, rather than aspire to be cleansed by it. I haven't raised you in the church and I probably won't now. When I make you go, you both make clear that I am making you go. You seem to enjoy it when you're there, but maybe that's just wishful thinking on my part. I wonder if this isn't another area in which I have failed you when it comes to discipline. The choice was a difficult one, but it felt necessary at the time. Catholicism was reeling with its sin of sanctioning the abuse of children. I didn't like the idea of placing you before such a corrupt institution, making you its child without your consent. And then religious doctrines were so cruel everywhere I turned. I am like that woman I once saw, in a beauty shop on the South Side of Chicago, who stood on the sink and shouted:

"You not gon' tell me my God is prejudice."

But that is precisely what is so often sold. I have since thought that isn't exactly true. There are faiths to belong to that don't contradict our values: Ifa, Bahai, Buddhism . . . Maybe those will become yours. Or maybe you will be like me, a person who cuts and pastes what she needs and who accepts a communing with the gospel in a church that is plagued with all the sins of the world.

And besides all that, I really did want you to choose how you would speak to God, if at all. I didn't want to make you do it in a particular way, just to be open to the gift of prayer. I couldn't promise it would give you what it has given me. In the hopes attached to instruction, people tell children all kinds of lies. "You should always do your best," for example, is a bad piece of advice. You will fall apart in exhaustion if you try to follow that goofy mantra. I try to tell more truth than that. But telling the complete truth isn't always so wise either. It can heap too many burdens on your shoulders. I mean, we don't watch the news in our house on a daily basis for a reason.

One great gift of the way of religion is that it trains you in ways of making sense of the ups and downs. Especially the devastating things that come into every life. Even when I find the doctrines unreasonably cruel, I like that about it.

But other things I don't like. And not just the judgmental doctrines. I don't like sayings like "If God wanted it for me it would be mine." I mean, the good part is that it is a mantra of nonattachment, a way of letting go of a fixation on particular things or people. But it also puts the whims of a fickle humanity into a divine order that I simply don't believe should bear that responsibility. Some things you won't get because people can be cruel or stupid. Some things won't happen because of error or mistake. I'm not putting that on God.

What I really want you to know is that life's task is to strike the right balance between aspiration and resignation, your responsibilities to the world, your communities and loved ones, and to yourself. Know that the cage is wrong and why the caged bird sings. These are the kind of gospels I embrace. Take joy in simple pleasures even as you pursue big dreams. Live in the along. Seek love and passion unceasingly. I could say other specific things about vegetables and sleep and cleaning yourself, but those all fit under those larger ethical banners. Stay away from charming narcissists, ambitious people with a dearth of imagination, and anyone who wants to use you to make themselves feel worthy when they feel unworthy. They are dangerous.

So, this is my alternative to imposing a particular religion on you. But then, of course, and this is the ever-present double-edged sword of progressive parenting, I have created a context in which some of our most conflicted interactions are over faith. So many things that I chose not to question in favor of transcendent faith are things you question and challenge, and it bothers me. That is good for me. It reminds me that children are not extensions of the parent. And that I have chosen for you to fly instead of staying in line. I am not raising you to be my creation but to be yourself. And I have seen the face of your spirituality. I have seen it most when you are in

the ocean for hours on end. Standing in front of all that vastness, laughing and playing. At those moments, I have wanted
to tell you to be like Emerson, "Make your own Bible. Select
and collect all those words and sentences that in all your reading have been to you like the blast of a trumpet."[7] And yet I
cannot underestimate the importance of community.

Religious education in the Society of Friends seemed
like the only thing I could commit to for you when it came
to church. And so, you have spent your lives in Quaker
schools, like I did in my elementary years. Weekly meetings
for worship, mostly silent except for when the spirit moves.
It is a faith ritual that is typically untethered from doctrine
beyond a belief that God is in everyone and in the virtue of
peace. The rest will have to come in time, with critique and
contemplation. And yes, growing up is a conversion in itself.

It is a conversion experience in which you choose what
and who you will emerge as from the chrysalis. Yes, I believe you choose, albeit within the constraints of wounds
and desire and the spectrum of possibilities in front of you,
of course. How will you treat your word? How will you hold
your heart? How will you hold others'? These are questions
in the path of becoming, that unbecoming process that is
gangly, pimpled, flailing, weeping. In the thicket of the
process of becoming there is always the threat of bumbling
awkwardness, and spectacular failure. But you must still go
through it, gathering new names for yourself along the way,

a palimpsest of existence. And when you emerge, you will understand it is not what you are called but what you answer to. That is your name.

I worry that you will find yourself bound by a misnaming. Bound by evil forces and lies. You are remarkable boys, but we are all at risk of falling under the sway of a much too cruel world. Maybe that's why I think so much about you flying, because upward bound is a direction and not the gallows.

In popular novels about ancient Chinese kingdoms there are often long passages about foot-binding. These books are usually both orientalist and fantastical. I, with a bit of embarrassment, love them. I know they emphasize strangeness and decadence in ways that are often problematic, but they are also so beautiful. And I am a sucker for descriptive beauty and melodrama. These novels have made me curious about foot-binding. And so, I looked up pictures. The images hurt my heart. Those toes that turn into the middle of the foot, did they turn numb or continue to ache? Wrapped so tightly, they refused spontaneous growth. The aspiration of perfect beauty that created ugliness haunts. These distended feet are the result of hampered existence, of gender as destruction. Elite women, held captive by their status and gender, bore this particular burden.

And then I wonder, what happened when, in a cultural upheaval, these self-same women were told foot-binding was over? And they could barely walk. And they saw those beautiful, free wide feet, toes wiggling, bodies planted solidly on the ground. Binding is an indebted attachment. It is not the same as promise, which is always contingent. It doesn't let you get free without serious wounding.

I hate when people do what I just did. Read an entire meaning into a culture and history that are unfamiliar to them beyond a particular form of popular and fantastic representation. But I did it for a reason. Because, despite my flat-footed (no pun intended) description of the practice of foot-binding, the metaphor is important. Be careful to what you are bound. Otherwise, you might author your own bitterness and bile.

Root doctors of the Old South could fix people so they would become bound to another. Binding was not the work of igniting passion. It was coercive, forcing someone to be locked into a relationship, an erasure of will. It was a trap, not love. Learning the difference is harder than it seems. We make idols of what draws us, of our desire to have the things that makes other think we are of value.

Stay free of that. Bind to that which and whom merits your love.

Whiteness is a potent form of binding. And there is something wild-eyed about whiteness right now, at this moment in history, and it is all about the coffers and to whom they belong. The drug that says that whiteness is what matters most about white people is what makes so many of them think that is what must be protected at all costs. Your self is not to be jealously guarded because it makes you superior. It is to be guarded because it is yours.

And yet, you cannot rely on certain expectations as Black people. You cannot say to yourself: If I do A, B, and C, then D will happen. It just doesn't work that way. What you put in may not have its just reward. But maybe it will. So, you have to have an inside thermometer, or better yet a barometer, of who you want to be and how well you are doing. Am I running hot or cold? Or am I in my pocket? In my bag? In my feelings? You already have it; it is the headstrong thing that sometimes puts people off. It is your necessary armor.

The Antillean revolutionary intellectual Frantz Fanon wrote about a third-person consciousness, the demand for Black people to always look at themselves from the outside in. He followed W. E. B. Du Bois, who wrote about a double consciousness, a form of second sight created by the doubleness of being an American and an African American, two warring selves in one body. I prefer my mother's wisdom regarding how you deal with racism: "Render them invisible." I told her that I couldn't do it in response, until I learned how and I realized it is a magical thing. Some things can be noticed and evaporated almost immediately for the sake of your own sanity and well-being. Practice it; it is a useful discipline. Of course, you balance that practice with understanding the world you occupy, to move about it with a healthy skepticism and abundant knowledge about how it works and how it wounds, and also how it rewards. But I'd hate for you to spend too much time outside yourself. Protect your insides. That's the point.

People want to truncate you. It happens to all of us human beings. We are victims of the shorthand schemas people use to organize the world. There's no real way around it. Sometimes you will make a bold statement, claiming the fullness of your being, and it will feel essential and groundbreaking. And then you will walk outside, or inside, and be reminded that the shortcut is back. As unpleasant as it is, keep in mind that life is so full of information. The shorthand shortcut is something we all do to manage things. But you do not have to submit to the shorthand that would make you a fiction. Claim your own summary, your own pithy capture of the ocean of who you are. And still, never mistake the shorthand for your whole self. Be ready to metamorphize when necessary.

One part of the shorthand is the amplification of the mistake, especially the big ones. It happens in our minds, and it also happens in the logic of race. Generations past were hypervigilant about the power of the single mistake. It could hurt the whole race. I am glad we are largely unburdened from that belief, even though the smallest mistake still has the potential to become so amplified that it can destroy your life as a Black person. It takes on outsized meaning for us as a result. Maybe one day you will break a law: steal a thing, trespass, cheat. And you will have to deal with the fact. And both live with it and move beyond it. If you become bound to your errors, you never get to work with them or through them. They remain a thousand cuts instead of the malleable scar tissue that we all need. Even if the slings and arrows come your way, cultivate your scar tissue. Massage it, clean it, tend to it.

When you both were little, we used to watch *The Wiz* over and over. It was one of our rituals. And we played the songs in the car. You asked for "Mean Ole Lion," Issa. You scowled and smiled and showed your little claws from your car seat. *The Wiz* is a coming-of-age story. The characters talk a journey into their futures and reencounter their pasts, seeking a way to return home, renewed. On the way, friendship and danger are constant companions. There are body snatchers hiding everywhere. Dorothy and her friends get caught by Evillene's motorcycle-driving flying monkeys.

The thing that saves them is Dorothy's ingenuity. And water! Evillene melts. Her prisoners are freed.

All small children have terrors. But yours are as real as they are mythic. Your monsters are not pretend. And they are old. They haunt. They hunt. The stories of what can happen are, in your minds, a true fiction. I think that is why we watched *The Wiz*. It is a hero's tale suited specifically for Black children.

Freeman, at the tender age of the tooth fairy, you kept having shark teeth. Your mouth wouldn't let go of the baby ones, and your body kept growing the adult ones. And so, you had to get the baby ones pulled. One of the worst moments of my parenting life was standing while you cried as the dentist pried out a tooth. She said it shouldn't hurt, but clearly it did. She stopped and gave you more medicine, but by that point you were shaking. It was awful. I should have stopped it. I didn't.

The next time I made sure they gave you a stronger anesthetic. This time you were giggly. As we took the elevator up to our apartment, you said to an elderly woman, while laughing, "How come there are two of you?" I laughed as well. She was unnerved.

The tooth situation was stressful for me. The first time I took you to the dentist, I hadn't been to one myself for twenty years, and I had some odd superstition that explained why I had a perfectly straight, cavity-free smile. But

I had to learn better, by trial. Issa, one day running fast and cheerful as usual, you crashed into a wooden play kitchen. Your tooth was distended, turned sideways. The dentist said that it had to be pulled, otherwise it would rot and ruin how your adult tooth would grow in. She pulled it. And afterwards you sobbed. "I want my tooth back." It took three years to return. And you still smile for pictures with your mouth closed.

George Washington's false teeth were not wood, as you may have heard. They were actually made from a variety of materials, including Black humans' teeth. The father of our country stole our teeth. Our bite. Think about that. What did Washington feel and think when the dentist inexpertly shoved Africans' teeth into his mouth. Was it the anxious trepidation one feels with a sloppy technology, or just one in many rituals of taking every bit of use value from the African? Did they pull them off cadavers, like entitled grave robbers, or was it a form of torture? One of the many rituals of slavery?

In an 1887 newspaper there was an article about a Philadelphia man who relished the lustrous shoes made from the skin of an African. "Is the down-trodden African still beneath your feet?" he was asked. In the most matter-of-fact way, and with the shadow of a smile, he answered: "I suppose you mean to inquire if I still wear shoes made of the skin of a negro. I certainly do, and I don't propose changing in that respect until I find a leather that is softer and will last longer and present a better appearance."[8]

Maybe your anguish and bloodcurdling screams at the dentist were all about the way history rides inside us our whole lives. The fear of body snatchers is warranted. It is an epigenetic terror, the threat of losing one's wholeness in the face of violence. I know having your teeth pulled by responsible dentists is nothing like that. But the way my heart screams at every hurt and slight you face has everything to do with the stalking body snatchers of the past and present. Even my illnesses, autoimmune ones, are the hallmarks of an inherited vigilance. Protectiveness run amok, so wild I wind up hurting myself. I hope I don't hurt you with it.

There are two infamous penitentiaries in the South. They are Parchman Farm in Mississippi and Angola Farm in Louisiana. OK, there are more than two. But the lore of these two are greatest, and the point is better made with specificity. The conditions on that loamy earth, that swampy land, that remote colonized echo of Africa are hardly changed from slavery days. At Parchman Farm, one of the greatest folklorists, Alan Lomax, collected the blues. He recorded the men talking, strumming, and singing; working too. There were a host of great bluesmen imprisoned at Parchman. I think of them, with their few precious hours for leisure, working their fingers nimbly over the strings. Many people don't know, picking cotton is hard on the fingers.

It requires dexterity and speed. The last thing, one might assume, that a cotton picker would feel like doing at night is work his or her fingers over hard strings. But the muscle required to manage the circumstance and its constraint was returned to in order to create beauty. Over and over again.

There is an interview with one man at Parchman who answers the question of what he did to get in there. He didn't do what he had been locked up for, but he figured he had done so much wrong, he was bound to get caught. It hurts my heart, the long-standing mismatch in Black life between deed and consequence. That sense of fate in his capture might have helped him make do, but the philosophy is wrong. The punishment does not, has not ever, fit the existence. Put yourself there: When dead magnolia blossoms hit the ground, their skirts fly open shamelessly. They turn from pink to a caramelized brown. You crush them underfoot and their stink sticks to the bottom of your shoe. The guitar, slung over your shoulder, is said with the accent on the first syllable. Work until your muscles cramp, the sweat has a life of its own, dancing, merging, splitting all over your body. It tickles the back of your head. Even there, in that body of the past, with the captivity of the present, there is a there there. We are still there.

If I cannot inoculate you to the way the terror and the hatefulness seep into your nervous system, your subconscious, your daily living, I do a racking with every ugliness.

A ritual exorcism. Only time will tell if it works. But just know that's the point of my mantras, of your genius, of your strength, of your greatness.

I think I am orchestrating your futures as I parent. But the truth is, you teach me who you are much better than I teach you who I think you should be. You have insisted I listen as an act of care. Even when I want to preach and profess. You insist I live by my word to care. Listening is care. You insist to me reminders that you are the engineers of your own lives. Not me. I am just to feed and nourish you, to make space for you to feed yourself.

Just always remember: even if you stumble again and again, you must move towards freedom. Even if you stumble again and again.

Freeman, your voice is Black. It sits at the lower register, like thunder, so deep sometimes I cannot hear you even when I can feel its reverberation. Issa, your voice, now, is high. You hate to be mocked. But your trilling is gorgeous. People have likened your singing voice to a young Michael Jackson's. Together you are like Paul Robeson singing "Swing Low, Sweet Chariot." A rumbling vibrato, a sweep into the air, dipping onto the field, the arms of angels coming to bring the forsaken up in the bosom of comfort.

I want you to ride the wind. Heed your senses. They remind us that we are inside our bodies but also outside of ourselves. Like when a breeze invites you to follow scent trails: Burning wood, honeysuckle, lavender. Cut grass. And then your allergies hit. They ruin the romance. It's funny. Then it's miserable. Once when I was with Auntie Michelle in Atlanta, we took the MARTA to Little Five Points to eat at the Jamaican restaurant there. It required us to walk through a field of grass. By the time we got to the other side, our eyes were swollen and red, and liquid ran from every opening on our heads. Benadryl became more appealing than veggie patties, and the result of all that was that we (and we have done this more than once) slept away most of the weekend adventure. It happens. Another time Auntie Farah called me and said, "Where are you?" and I answered, "Oh! I'm walking through a field in South Carolina." It was more vacant than bucolic. She laughed. It also made her a bit worried. Not because of the allergy potential (I am not allergic to South Carolina the way I am allergic to Georgia), but because all of our imaginations are haunted by Southern woods. But like Brer Rabbit said, we were born and bred in the briar patch; navigating danger is our lot, and despite everything, we have done quite well as fugitives.

The quiet hum of a nebulizer, a lifeline for asthmatics, is a common sound in the Black American home. Like the sharp puff of an inhaler. Midnight coughs. A steaming bathroom. When I slept with an oxygen tank because I just couldn't seem to suck up enough air, I waited until you went to bed to turn it on. I didn't want to scare you. The desperate panic of breathlessness is a chain, a link from the ship's hold to asbestos-dusted hallways, jet-black mines, and the grip of a cop's arm. No wonder, then, that an art would come of controlling the breath, of tumbling words, of time, of mastery of the split second of inhalation and a spray of magnetic spray of release—an edifice, a castle, a landscape. The rapper knows the exercise. Respiration is more than survival. It is dancing at the crossroads.

I used to dream, in childhood, about being chased, breathlessly, by the Klan through the woods. I think it came from watching *Roots* when I was in kindergarten. I suppose that's why I wasn't so into the woods when I was small. But at some point, my senses took over and I yearned for the drunkenness of nature's smells and sounds; even the way some grasses you feel inside your ears, and I have no idea how that happens. Deep in the woods, when there is a canopy above me, I think about how our street in Birmingham used to be like that. There was a canopy of trees in the summertime that kept the street not exactly cool but not so hot.

Remember when you used to watch the TV show *Wild Kratts*, about animals? And there was that episode that talked about animals that live life in the canopy, riding the top? I found that interesting, but if we were nonhuman animals, I think it would be better to do as we do as humans. We can climb, which means we can ride the top and plunge the depths.

This is why I write. And why I sometimes fail at little everyday things, like cleaning out the car and the kitchen every night. Yes, I love to cook for you and give you cozy blankets and hug you a great deal and the smell of freshly folded laundry. But my domesticity sometimes falls short because I want to show you how I'm pursuing the thing I have claimed that I want you to have: freedom. Please remember that.

Fortune

I was embarrassed by boys like Flynn. He, in his cut-off jean shorts, narrow from the top of his head, to his knobby knees and toe joints, would make sure I had a seat every time we rode on the city buses. He smiled, brilliant teeth underneath clay lips the same earthen color as his skin. Flynn was always ashy, and yet his skin was always pretty anyway. He wasn't suave. He was jingly voiced and sincere. I didn't like him offering me a seat. I was embarrassed that he thought I ought to be tended to. But I smiled back and I said no thank you. Unlike with many boys, I couldn't be super-fluously nasty to him. I don't know where I got that from.

He was a sweet, gentle Chicago boy. And he was not a boy who broke glass.

In Gwendolyn Brooks's poem "Boy Breaking Glass," the boy, whose inheritance has been robbed, shouts, "I shall create! If not a note, a hole. If not an overture, a desecration." This disaster is the consequence of a frustrated manhood. Brooks recognizes rage. "It was you who threw away my name! And this is everything I have for me."

I have wondered to whom he spoke. To the air? Who listened to the weight of his anguish? Miss Fortune, the cruel lady of exclusion, is an emotional boomerang. She teaches you to throw the brick out of your yard and injure yourself.

I am always dropping glasses. And I notice this—the shards scattered about the ground are beautiful. They catch light; they have an organic geometry. I have learned over time and by experience, however, that if I don't clean the mess up entirely, we will be bleeding all over the place. Or digging shards out of our feet. And so I brush the glass into the dustbin until the sound moves from tiny tinkles to the softest swish. Until the shards are too small to sweep, and I pick them up by pressing my masking-taped hand against the floor in every corner.

The shards of heartbreak cannot simply be thrown away. They have to be reworked. This requires a careful examination, a tender holding. Of whoever is broken, whether it is you or someone you love.

———

You know a woman became a mother. You will know a mother is a woman.

I remember exactly what I was wearing. I was fifteen. I had a jumper on. And a coral-colored midriff top. And bangs. And a long ponytail. I loved how I looked that day. I'd seen him before. Like other boys, he grabbed my wrist. It happened on the train, in the mall. Sometimes they fell to their knees, playing, and said, "Will you marry me?" I didn't understand any of it and, to be honest, wasn't sure why they were doing what they were doing. I was naïve.

This time, when I saw him I said,

"I know you!"

He could speak. But he was mute. That was the first sign something was awry. His smile was sickly, sickening. Before I knew it, his hands were around me, and traveled, and I hated myself for wearing that top. And I fought. And I said, "I don't know you."

And when the train came in, and my face was on the concrete, they all looked away from me and boarded. And he said he should kill me. And pressed my head into the floor. I could hear the strands of my straightened hair snapping. My scalp scraping. The ting of my earring, and then a scrape. That was all so close, and me trying to keep my skirt down felt miles away.

Whatever the affection was had turned to rot, or was rotten to the core from the outset. I learned later he wasn't well. He spent his days riding the trains. If I saw him get on a train, I would get off, no matter the stop. One week when it happened three times, I decided to stop riding the trains for a while altogether.

He was wounded and so was I.

My father wanted to settle things the Brooklyn way. He planned to roam the street with a baseball bat. Men who love me, at various moments, have imagined settling things this way whatever the affront or abuse. They want to beat dudes' asses. And I must admit it has been something of a comfort, but it reminds me of how contorted they are in pain at my suffering and how love, ultimately, demands more. That you stand in front of your pain, your helplessness, sometimes.

And the truth is, much worse has happened to millions of women and men. Worse has even happened to me. Sometimes children witness these terrors. I know, for a child, it can be world-collapsing to see the vulnerability of those who protect you. So, this is a lesson I want to approach tenderly, but also seriously. Because I believe that if you're going to be decent, you cannot turn a blind eye to me or to others. Nor can you simply strike out in rage. Because, really, the whole point of the crisis is exactly there. People make others eat their grief and rage. You are never to make others eat your rage, no matter how often you are told that is what it means to be a man and that is the source of dignity. It is important to understand that some things that are described as part of being a man in this world are beneath your promise and beauty. They are beneath all of us.

You must not hold another's face on the concrete even if you find yourself shattered or shattering.

This means you must forgive yourself for your failures. Pushing someone into the concrete comes in some large measure from hating who you are and punishing those who know it. Choose accountability over shame. Now I'm telling you to do something that is un-American and not masculine. Because Americans are addicted to innocence. That is part of its parsimoniousness with respect to democracy. They are never held to account, like the child with donut crumbs around her mouth who is so cute we pretend to believe she didn't swallow the sugar. Masculinity denies weakness. Americanness is a bully and baby at once.

Boys must know about hurt. Boys do know about hurt. They know these things. They do these things, but they also endure them. And suppress them so much that they forget. The time for unearthing is always now. Witness your beloved. Sit with your own hurt. I have to say this, explicitly, because

I recognize my own hypocrisy at work. I have always wanted you to be deeper and wider than the scope of prescribed masculinity. But I bought you the toys and clothes prescribed for boys from the outset. The one exception was a baby boy doll who wore a green jumpsuit. I bought him because I wanted you to learn to nurture. But other than that it was trucks and blocks and Legos. Maps and globes. So, I worry that I must tell you about tendernesses that perhaps you could have seen for yourself had I set things before you differently.

Have you thought much about maps? They remind you how easy it is to misperceive and believe the order of things must be as they are. When I was seven years old, the globe in my classroom at school had Rhodesia written clearly in Southern Africa. I told my teacher, Risa, that the name of the country was Zimbabwe. Rhodesia was a colonial name; Zimbabwe was the people's choice. I had overheard the political conversations among my parents and their friends.

Risa, to her credit, taped over the word "Rhodesia" with "Zimbabwe." I felt like I was doing my part for the revolution. Changing something. When you turn a map upside down, flipped from the way you are accustomed to seeing it, it looks odd. When you do things your own way, the same thing happens. But you should always experiment. Flip the map. See what happens. Know that it can all be understood another way, even if you ultimately live inside convention. I want you to know that it all can be seen a different way.

Mema's car was a gold Dodge Dart. It only had an AM radio. I don't remember if we were rear-ended or if we rear-ended another. My face slammed into the dashboard and blood began spilling out. That day I kept telling her, "I'm OK. I'm OK, don't worry." The consequence of this fender bender was mostly nothing, I thought. Until I was twenty-one and learned that my jaw was hollow. After the hit, a cyst had grown, making the bone paper thin. A punch could have shattered it. Trauma is like that. It can hollow you out. It can wound and disorder. An extrinsic injury becomes something that echoes inside you.

I cannot protect you from every wound. But in giving you the stories of my body, I want to show you something about care and healing. Which is what you must devote your life to in large part. Living is hard. People are lying to you if they tell you they refuse to submit to random humiliation. It is incessant and, yes, especially for us Black people. You try not to swallow it, even though raising a voice of protest every time is deeply impractical. As you cross the street and a driver revs up, laughing, you submit but don't swallow. It is the cashier who overlooks you. It is the professional peer who refuses to call you by your title. The ones who give you condescending instructions presuming your ignorance or incompetence. Their faces of surprise when you open your mouth and speak their language eloquently. The insult is incessant. But when you name it, they spin another story of hypersensitivity and hysteria. Like the truth is a breaker for outrage.

Proselytize this: calling all Black people from the ocean floor, the grand earth, the digested fecal matter turned over to murderous guards, the tended graves, the unmarked, the unnamed, the stolen, the thieves. You need a practice of reconstitution, of filling up your font. Of cleansing the stench of humiliation, to face it another day without being defeated.

Issa, I remember when you began to have nosebleeds. You were a toddler. And one day you toppled down the stairs. After that the nosebleeds came regularly, every couple of months. Rapid rivulets of bloodstream. A nosebleed is terrifying and mundane at once. Almost everyone gets them, but when you cannot stanch the flow, the panic in your chest makes you worry: Will I wait too late to get help if I don't go now? Will I go woozy and lose consciousness? Will it ever stop? Will you be OK if I'm not there to hold your head back and your back straight?

These are forward-looking questions: about what to do now, in anticipation for what we do not know. Fortune-tellers can't predict what will devastate you, what will make your blood run cold. What will save you. When blessings will flow or burdens will crack you.

In the meantime, don't forget to enjoy the small things in small moments. Like the pleasure of drinking through a straw. Or smooth sheets. Or a hug. It really does feel like the end of history now. We worry about the impending destruction of the earth. The constant loop of the past in the present with social media. The way nothing ever stops. The ever-present mantra of never again and the over and over again of the greatest human cruelties. We are in now and then at once. But there still is a future, as harrowing as it might be. I admit. I try to give you everything in the face of this. Every bit of sweetness. To indulge and spoil. To delight. There is enough of the other stuff for everyone's lifetimes a million times over.

My parents would cut out letters from wrapping paper and tape them above my bed to wish me a happy birthday. I looked forward to waking up every year, every birthday. Then we would go to Dispensa's Kiddie Kingdom with my friends and delight in raggedy old rides in a quaint amusement park. Every year I got terribly nauseated on the Tilt-A-Whirl, and yet I couldn't resist it.

In more mundane weeks my mother would sew my dresses and alter my clothes herself. She made my curtains too. She let me pick out the fabric, ricrac, and lace. And then she let me use some of the fabric to sew dresses for my Barbie dolls. I thought I would have a daughter to whom I would pass on my collection of Black dolls, from Germany and the

Caribbean, handmade dolls and those by Mattel. Ones with Afros, and ones with silky straight hair that hung to their waists. Dolls whose clothes you could change, and ones who would pee if you put their mouths under the faucet.

My mother had told me the story, growing up, of her younger sister Barbara, who received the gift of a Black doll. It was a rare and wondrous thing for a Black girl from a working-class family in the segregated South. It was beautiful; it was also cruel. The others made dolls of pipe cleaners and Coke bottles. Bobby had one that looked like her. My mother made sure, when she had the chance, that I would have many that looked like me.

If you had really wanted a bunch of dolls, I would have given them to you. But I didn't of my own accord, because for a feminist, I was awfully attached to gender conventions. And I was afraid at first that because you were boys, you would pull further away from me than a girl would. But that is not a foregone conclusion. Gender isn't foregone at all. And even though you have both easily donned the mantle "boy," I now know that it doesn't have to be what it has been taken to be, in identity or connections to others, or between us. That is a matter of the relationships we have. You are both excellent critics of sexism. Freeman, in the third grade you commented on the sexism of a story the class was reading. The teacher, perhaps thinking you didn't know what you meant, asked why you thought it was sexist. You explained that the woman was being valued for her beauty and nothing else. The man was fixated upon her, but didn't bother to know her. Issa, you called my refusal to let you pierce your ears inconsistent with my feminist identity. "If I was a girl, you know you would let me get my ears pierced. You say it is cultural, but it's just gender rules." True. "Culture," I have said, but of course nearly everything terrible is part of culture as much as that which is good. Culture isn't a word that ought to work as a defense. Be better than me with respect to that.

Years ago, a colleague who I could not stand said to me: You're a closet conservative, you're always citing the Bible. He was wrong and as usual exercising his sole intellectual habit: provocation. And doing so poorly. I am not a conservative of any stripe. But I do seek divine wisdom. But trying to make you unfettered, I didn't baptize you. Yes, I'm saying this again because it is a worrisome thing for me. Around when you were born, I began to feel such distress in religion. The growth of fanaticism, the violence of certainty in belonging to a chosen few, the self-righteous condemnation of others, the disparate responses to evil, the othering of "others." I did not want to make you think it was good to believe any of that. Moreover, knowledge, questioning, inquiry, and challenge are good. What religion has become in the current social landscape, for the most part even if not completely, is a boondoggle that confounds knowledge. So, I left you free of it for the most part. And still the spirit stays close to you like white on rice. And the truth is, I feel God in the celebration of Mass. And if I had my druthers, you would too. I feel the sentence "Jesus is my personal savior" ring true to me, even as I know it doesn't mean to me what it means to so many others. For me, it means that the story of Christ is my ethical anchor. And the ritual allows me to access a poetry beyond the word. I wasn't sure if it would do the same for you. Perhaps I have failed to equip you with something I believe is, if not necessary, potentially quite good. The point of religion, as I take it, as I find it meaningful, is that it gives us powerful metaphors for confronting our experience of the divine. But that isn't all it is. It is also community. My ambivalence towards communities is perhaps my greatest flaw. But I don't want to be that way. I don't want you to be that way. Because we need others, deeply.

One day I open up Facebook and I see that a former student of mind has made a digital picture of me with you, Freeman, when you were a baby. But he thinks you are Issa. It is a Madonna and child photo, so that is apt, as "Issa" is the Arabic word for "Jesus." He draws us in blue and reddish brown. He gives us golden halos. That day, Issa, you are reading Coleridge's "Rime of the Ancient Mariner" aloud to me, and when you read the line "Nor dim nor red, / like

God's own head, / The glorious Sun uprist," I tell you it is a metaphor for the halo around God's head in religious iconographic paintings.[3] Such moments of kismet always feel like messages from the ancestors to me.

When they happen, I pray at my altar. It is an invitation for the saints to feast and a supplication for grace, a praise song for you. I have many things there: amulets of endurance and shape-shifting, Ganesha, Oxóssi, Madonna and child, symbols of Shintoism and hoodoo. I cantillate the rosary. I love Christ—he cast himself with the poor and downtrodden and reviled. He sacrificed for humanity. He directs you where to offer your moral attention. But the church and Christians are often not Christ-like. I've needed more. I storm through the passions of faith by feel. I have explained to you why Kali is there, the Hindu goddess, often Black, who stands in the midst of death and destruction, her lolling tongue and shining dark body terribly alive. Why Oshun, the Yoruba goddess of love, clad in yellow, lover of honey and watermelon, sweetness and the river waters, is there. I like my spirit life tactile and complicated and full of symbol and mystery. And that is also the why of the coiling thread of smoke. The wafture. You can touch them, though the scent is sharper than the gossamer smoke. Prayers written and folded at home and elsewhere: In Notre Dame in Paris. In a temple in Japan. In a church in Bahia. They're always for you but also for me. For us.

That is another answer to the question why I don't go to church even though I do love church. Because I respond to everything that feels like God. Living is church. It is my birthright, I think. A child of the fragments. A Catholic mother and grandmother, a Primitive Baptist great-grandmother, a Jewish father, a Lutheran birth father, a mother's mother's mother's mother somewhere back for whom fetishes were the way rosaries are for me. It is the collage of spirituality. Ragtag yet ceremonial. I come from a broken home. We broke your home. You are the children of divorce. But I do not think of it as tragedy. It is more like Gil Scott-Heron's story in the song-poem "On Coming from a Broken Home." His story, told from the inside out, is not the story the law and policy tell of brokenness. Instead, it is a story of marrow-deep love and the bindings of wisdom and responsibility and, most of all, a Southern grandmother's spirit that lifted everyone inside her home.

I love that song. He knew, I know, brokenness, according to the legal conventions of the world, is not the same thing as spirit brokenness. It is not even family brokenness. We can make beautiful collages out of the shards, like the Japanese Kintsugi pots that, after shattering, are glued back together, the fault lines reattached by veins of gold and silver. Family is what you make of it. So is love. And so, I pray at a fragmented altar. There are two statuettes of a Black Madonna and child. One for each of you, I suppose. I pray

for you there. Sometimes my prayers say: I do not want
something to happen to you. I do not want you to do this.
But more often they are about how you face whatever comes.
I am not an oracle. I seek answers even in the absence of
the power of divination. And yet I hope to be a vessel, one
of those ancient women who classicist Walter Burkert described as "frenzied women from whose lips the god speak."[4]

So many came before. That is the mother's legacy from
whence I come. Praying women. At one point in my life I
attempted to pray unceasingly, constantly saying the rosary
to myself at the back of my mind. Living as prayer. I think
that is when I am at my best. Because seeing through prayer
provides a remarkable clarity. Not in the doctrinal sense,
but because it is, at best, the lens of a love for every tattered
inch of this earth.

You both have the eyes I had before one of my diseases
made mine bulge out. Sometimes I get so sad about the
bulging. I look in the mirror and I think I have turned into
a Topsy-like character. But not really. It is not that I don't
like big eyes; it is that I still wish I had my eyes. But at least
I have given them to you. They are deep set and so dark
as to appear black. They are shaped like almonds. Issa you
have told me, "You used to have our eyes. But now yours
are *huge*!" And make it seem like something good. But you,
you have the gaze of depth. To see outside from an interior
depth, that is a metaphor and a state of grace.

As a mother, I try to give you what you need. I try to always be strong and capable, to make sure you feel protected under my wings. But sometimes I fail. I am terrified of mice. I know it is a cliché. It is one of my greatest weaknesses. It is a phobia in the literal sense. So, when they came into our house, during construction that was necessary because the facade just toppled off one day, I quaked in terror day and night. It was ridiculous and even funny in retrospect. I needed help with simple tasks. I wanted to throw my whole house away. We went to a virtually empty hotel in the middle of a snowstorm and as a result I wound up shoveling with a borrowed broom in the abandoned parking lot. I mean it was absurd. I felt inadequate and ashamed. I cried a lot. Then, when we were returning home from the hotel, the two of you stepped inside the house before me. You saw a mouse near a trap I had set. You sent me to the car and threw a box on top of it until the exterminator arrived. It was all so ridiculous, funny even, except for the fact that my feelings were as sober as a funeral. In those four weeks of hysteria, I saw the tables turn. That I actually would not always be strong. That you will try to give me what I need, even when I fail. That I would laugh, a lot, at my own absurdity and you would join in with me. That is love.

One day I received an email at 3 a.m. It read, "Imani, If you died tonight, would the family be alright?" No, they wouldn't. But they would survive. And not by virtue of the insurance policy being sold in the email, something I already had. Don't they know I am Black, I wondered? Don't they collect all that kind of demographic data so they know how to entice and humiliate me at once? Don't they know that I can scarcely imagine a life without financial disaster around the corner all the time, no matter how secure my professional ascent seems to be? The question of "will they be alright?" registers to me as something other than financial security. It is a question for me about enduring the heartbreak of a terrible loss. The sort of heartbreak that is always too proximate, too threatening.

Once, before my grandmother died, before my heart went in a tailspin that I have not fully recovered from, she was angry at an aunt. In the midst of the argument she said, "When I die, I'm gonna haunt you."

Well, I plan to haunt you boys, too, but not in a vengeful way. But rather in the way Mudeah haunts us. As a constant bolster. As a spirit guide. It might not be as a spectral presence. It might simply be as an inheritance. A noble one. I will pull you towards the map of genealogy. To New Orleans, to South Carolina . . . to fields and sweat and books and struggle, and making do.

I decried genealogy as soon as each of you were born. I met you after you were born. So, I knew had you not grown inside me, that also would have been true. To look at your faces, to hold your tiny forms, was a new and overwhelming love. I gave and give my body to you, of course. Genealogically but much more importantly as an act of love. I rocked you and changed you. I wake up early for you and lean over you. And I look at you when I have made you angry and cry. I witness. I give my body, my presence, and therefore my heart. Literally, it beats for you. And figuratively too.

So, when I speak of inheritance, I am not talking about a bloodline, although whatever that thing means, you have it. Inheritance, I think, seeps through proximity and works its way under flesh and into bone. This is how I am my father's child. And were you a changeling, like me, I would love you just as completely. I know.

When my father called me that day, he said, "I'm going to die today." I come from a family that laughs inappropriately. So, I laugh when I tell that story. Because it was so ridiculous and so much my father. And so horrible. Incontinence and pain and the certainty that he was at the end had made him decide that day would be the day of his death. But given how euthanasia is illegal, his matter-of-factness could not be executed.

He didn't want me to see him. I did. I flew there the next day. I held his hand. I took pictures of our hands clasped. His, only slightly squeezing mine, once or twice. As I flew back home, a few moments into the flight, my breath came up short; I couldn't catch it, my heart fluttered.

I landed and learned he was dead.

When I landed, and stepped into the car, and strapped myself in, I turned to the backseat and said to you, "Grandpa died."

Freeman, you said, "I knew. I knew you were going to say that."

Perhaps the sign had been that your annual ritual of watching fireworks sitting on top of the roof of his car hadn't happened that Fourth of July. At first, I thought the ritual was odd, since when I was little, you had never allowed me to celebrate the Fourth. And then I felt relieved. We all need a respite from our stridency as we age. It helps ease the pain of defeat. It was his time to rest; it is our time to struggle.

And that is your fortune. Your inheritance is not in the coffers. It is not doubloons and stocks. It is in the buried bones. You are heir to the skeletons, the vertebrae of unnamed heroes.

Some of you, readers, will understand why I say to Freeman that when you were tiny, about four or five, I felt great pride that you had learned not to leave any meat on the chicken bone. You suck the marrow, leaving a clean gray thing when you are done. And Issa, you have learned to spit out the fine white bones as we relish our fishing haul of porgies (called scup in New England) and when eating a catfish fried in cornmeal.

Mudeah loved that I gave you her family name as a middle name, Issa: Garner. It is a word that means "to earn."

Our people have done that in spades. More than once I have called you to the computer to look at the perfect cursive lists of ancestors who have been digitized into our view. I want you to look closely at the man who owns land but is illiterate. I want you to marvel about a man who could own all that land without being able to read and write. To know that kind of genius that reaches out no matter what is withheld. These are your bones, child. You decide.

Throwing the bones: it is a way to tell fortunes that happens all over the world, and which has been done for millennia. Sometimes the bones cast about are human bones or other animal bones or bone-like objects, like shells. They land in combinations that say certain things. Throwing the bones is sometimes done in hoodoo with an animal scapula. That is the bone that is shaped like a wing, the mark of flight that, denuded, scraped clean, is fit to tell a story. Freeman, you had what is medically called a winged scapula when you were young; you could jut it out and pull it back in. It was beautiful and a bit unnerving. An ability outside of what we usually know is safe.

In some traditions, cowrie shells, which symbolize abundance, are used for divination like bones. In Shintoism, it can be the shell of a turtle or revealed over a deliberate circumambulation around divine temples. I have shaken fortunes out of cylinders in Kyoto. Cee-lo, played with dice, is yet another game of chance rooted in geomancy. Dominos is also called "bones" in pockets of Black English. These are simply mimicries of spiritual speculation. Tools of intercession became games of chance, and the reverse is true as well. Remember when I got into the habit of playing scratch cards? It was thankfully brief. The plan was, I would keep playing as long as I won. And I did, $100 here, $50 here, until the last time when I broke even. I was only going to go as far as the luck went, and it wasn't so much about the money but rather, as I said, the pleasure of having the hot hands, knowing which button to press on that Pennsylvania State Lottery machine as though I could divine something that was surely no more than chance or dumb luck.

I have experienced the gift of divination with spiritual leaders more than once. In my experience, it is far more profound than the caricatured fortune-telling of our popular culture. No turbaned woman with an artificial Bulgarian accent sitting before a glass ball in which the clouds clear revealing a certain future, of grace or ill. No, instead it is a stripping down to fundamental lessons for one's life. And it is a mediation between the lives and loves that have gone and the ones right here with us, whether they are from our family tree or other forms of spiritual sustenance that came before us and give meaning to our lives today.

The dead speak after death. And when the flesh is gone off the human body, whether by means of decay or in the furnace of cremation, what is left is not only ash but the bones and teeth. It is the architecture of a life, the anatomy, that remains. And it is more than a metaphor to say that when we seek to make sense of what has gone before, in order to move into the future, we begin with slivers: beams, foundations, building blocks. We take these little stories and use them to see ourselves into what is going to come. So, when one reads the bones, as a spiritualist, artist, or simply a rooted person, it is a means of breathing life back into the past. It is a form of ancestor veneration in which one steps into their skin, a swimming libation, a holy masquerade. We reanimate what we have inherited, by hook or crook, by choice or chance, to seek guidance.

In the biblical story of the dry bones in the desert, God speaks to Ezekiel. He tells Ezekiel to prophesy to the bones, to tell them to hear the word of the Lord. God promises tendons, flesh, and viscera. He promises life to the prophet.

Ezekiel, heeding the word of the Lord, preaches. Under the wind of his breath, the bones jangled and clacked; they snapped together. Flesh—bloody, wet, pulsing—grew. The sounds, I imagine, of Ezekiel's holy conjure, were just like the sound of death. You may already know, that when you sit in vigil, as someone dies, you will hear a rattle coming from their chests. It is an otherworldly sound that makes everything around you feel as though it is happening in slow motion. What you know, in that whistle and clatter, is something that doesn't require a doctor to speak or a priest to bless, for you to trust your first mind, that this is their end.

Breathing life back into the past, pulling from the ranks of your history, is how you build yourself. You are born to something and someplace; you become of a living accord and road. This is how we move forward. Letting the constraints of the moment die a little bit, to breathe life into the process of becoming.

It might sound like it, but I'm not telling you boys to carry the burden of your ancestors' wildest dreams like the T-shirts frequently say. You have heard enough of that for multiple lifetimes. On your father's side, you have generations of achievement in the face of a vicious American white supremacy. There are portrait painters and physicians, teachers and preachers, race men and women. But even if those names were not in your family tree, they would be yours to draw upon. And I would tell you to, but I would refuse to let you only pick from those strands of your inheritance. You also need the ones of those whose fingers cotton cut and whose hands stayed empty even after working year in and year out to become a thickly calloused plane, yellow and with the lifeline almost faded.

On my side, you are descended from people who didn't go north when others did, people who stayed in the thick of violence and history. Who faced instead of fleeing, who endured rather than escaping. They made it by virtue of labor and wits, ring shouts and cosmograms, and always knowing more than they let on. This known life is one that isn't a steadily perfect ascent to new heights of something that is called the American dream but is really a cruel escape hatch that only takes a few. It is one in which you circle the sun, you cross over calendars, year after year, and even if you always end up where you began, you have made some real beauty of that time from the slick seal-skinned newborn to the crepe-paper forearm that will touch death's door (if you are lucky).

Cosmograms are one of many Southern Black connections to our Kongo past. They are drawn, on the ground, in the form of a cross or a diamond or a spiral. Around their perimeter are the markings of the four movements of the sun. For the Kongo people that is the sign of the cycles of our existence, and the connection across the border of life and death. The death rattle and the birth cry, the bones coming back to life—we witness this pathway, and in the interstitial moments we grow and build and continue to walk around in a circle, without a destination apart from living inside ourselves. I know it is annoying, but this is actually the reason I make you go on long walks that leave your feet aching. You've got to make your way around this place, flat footed, connected to the ground as your antennae reach up far beyond the tops of your natty heads.

And on this journey we find each of our lives, and each generation, at least since the world cracked up with violence, becomes the representation of this question: How can you be Black and witness this world? How can you be Black and testify to the truth, while holding the future aloft? I once asked you, Issa, after a class discussion about the civil rights movement, whether you told your teacher your people were from Alabama, and you said, "I didn't want to brag." I suspect you get it already. That knowing is your precious inheritance.

I don't like Christmas. I don't like the icy cold and the dark, short days. Perhaps it is because of my eldest uncle.

Boot died in 1948 at Christmastime. I do not know where he is buried. In 1948, rheumatic fever was the leading cause of death for children in the United States. It started as strep, but then inflammation spread all over, to the joints and muscles, to the heart and brain. The valves of the heart could wither. I have autoimmune diseases; I know a bit about what these things feel like. I cannot imagine them at nine years old. I cannot imagine you two, my children, with them.

I do not understand. I wonder. How did my grandmother continue? How did she become the woman who made my bathwater the exact temperature, just shy of scalding and warming to the bones, and my grits perfectly buttery, and who wiped my tears and sent me letters telling me my enemies would suffer threefold for every misdeed they cast my way? How did she not curdle into bitterness? Her first child died, and I do not know how she made it. But she did. My God, she did.

And she wasn't afraid to love any of the rest of us, even though the haunting of loss couldn't have ever left. And she taught us to be headstrong and outspoken and brilliant, to move forward even when forward, as she well knew, wasn't promised. And when my knees swelled like Boot's, she covered them with an electric blanket and told me stories of her childhood.

Boot died at Christmas, right before his tenth birthday.

I do not like Christmas, but as long as there is breath in my body, I will make it beautiful for you, with the presents of your dreams and brightly colored wrapping paper: Black Santas and teal dots and ribbon I curl by running it against the flat side of a pair of scissors with speed and confidence. I buy lots of treats, like key lime cake and frosted cookies. I am indulgent. But I remember the time my grandmother told me that one Christmas all she had to give her children was oranges. I remember once we came along one of the highlights of Christmas was peppermint sticks stuck into oranges. I remember the joyful chaos of Christmas in Birmingham, once everyone had enough to give every child a gift, and the living room, which we never were allowed to sit in otherwise, was filled with a thousand toys: Easy-Bake ovens, cap guns, and baby dolls. Our luxury and the jubilant faces of the children have always had meaning.

And yet I do not much like Christmas. I feel as though I mourn my way through it.

The only moments I really love at Christmastime, except for those few minutes when you happily open your gifts, are when the night is inky blue just beyond the windows that line our home, and we have strung hundreds of illuminated lights, which reflect in your eyes. And the lamps and ceiling lights have been shut. And those tiny dazzling colors land on your face and I can see that slash across your faces, the chiseling of your features, the scarification of a high cheekbone and a fine jaw. Because you are here with me, and you are each an ageless and timeless echo, much greater than any of us know.

I think of June Jordan, who always understood the intimacy between the deepest joy and the most mournful yearning.

She wrote:

> *The difference of our positions will show*
> *Stars in your window I cannot even imagine.*
> *Your sky may burn with light,*
> *While mine, at the same moment,*
> *Spreads beautiful to darkness.*
> *Still, we must choose how we separately corner*
> *The circling universe of our experience.*
> *Once chosen, our cornering will determine*
> *The message of any star and darkness we encounter.*[5]

I want you to follow the stars, where they take you, to go the way your blood beats, and once you are there, I want you to build a glorious edifice at the pitch of freedom so whole that you forget the skeleton and scaffold were ever necessary. We have a tradition that speaks of this: the North Star to freedom, the star that guided the wise men to the Messiah. Such lights shone in the midst of a warm, comforting darkness that will take you to find yourself. If I say, Follow your yearnings, that seems cliché, but it isn't. It is a sermon, though maybe a bit crude. And it has a particularly potent meaning for us. Because at the core of American racism is the belief that the things we the Blacks desire, the fact that we the Blacks desire, are perversions, either because we get too big for our britches or because our britches are too styled and tattered at once.

Desire is such a beautiful and mysterious thing. It is dangerous too. It coils around the world as it is. We are often driven by what we are told is the source of our loneliness, our feelings of inadequacy, our suffering. And the desire that grows can become a terrible distortion of the truth, a misunderstanding of our needs. We are also, however, driven by a yearning to be seen and understood. Sometimes that yearning is so strong we allow ourselves to be eaten up by it, by those who would exploit it. But at other times, the good times, it is what makes us leave here having done something of value.

Take the time to strip yourself down to the core, to the simplest of joys. What if you dream your life but remove all money moves, all contingent material fantasies? And just fill it with connection, grace, and rituals? How would it be? What would it look like? That isn't an ascetic's dream so much as it is gospel of living in the along. It is a ritual of reorientation, a steadying, a sense of grace. It might not be enough, but it is something. And the fact is, if you get desire right, you will probably get love right too.

Easter is my favorite holiday. From the sacrifice of Lent, to the passions of the cross and the vigil, to Resurrection

Sunday. And at that moment of the new beginning we all glisten in seersucker and linen. Our faces gleam with moisture. We step outside to share finery, an annual promenade. You can even bring candy in to Mass and let a little stick to your pants leg by accident. I love that the sun is usually shining, and families with children are often late. And we sing, "He arose, with a mighty triumph over his foes. He arose a victor from the dark domain, and he lives forever with his saints to reign." I suppose you have heard me, off-key, smiling, a bit too animated for someone who is not in the choir and fails at carrying a tune. But I am gleeful. And yes, I know you both find it mostly boring except for the baskets and a little bit of the singing, and even those are losing their charm. But I will keep taking you because I know you will need *it* even if not precisely this way: something in the wake of all this death; the eternal spring.

Afterword

Our inner lives are eternal, which is to say that our spirits remain as youthful and vigorous as when we were in full bloom. Think of love as a state of grace, not the means to anything, but the alpha and the omega. An end in itself.

—GABRIEL GARCÍA MÁRQUEZ[1]

Since this may be the only life
it is sensible to make it full and alive
and rich and satisfying

—DENNIS BRUTUS[2]

Would you be interested in writing a book that is a letter to your boys?

That is how this book began, with a question from my wonderful editor, Gayatri Patnaik. I had a habit of talking about my sons on social media. I have also written them letters since they were infants. I know the power of letters. I have received and written them my whole life. The answer was easily yes.

I could have done something else. I could have also written one to the kind of children I don't have: girls. What would I have said to girls? Much the same. Maybe with more words about not letting yourself be eaten up by love. Or maybe a child who rejects gender categories wholly? I could have written to them instead, and in truth the lessons would be virtually the same. But my sons are real in my life, and this is really for them. But know, also, if I had had your child instead of mine, the heart of what I said would repeat, though its elaboration moved by circumstance.

I also realized that the invitation entailed a risk. There would be judgment of my errors. And far more importantly, my children, though agreeing at first, might grow to resent it. They are both gifted writers, so if that is the case, or if not, I hope their own words about coming of age make it onto pages, whether it is in diaries or books. I hope they can make space where I have failed, speak truths that I may have failed to gather, to answer back to me when I am wrong.

Notwithstanding the risk, I decided to write it anyway, because for me, the call to craft grew so much stronger after I became a steward of my sons' lives. What I had to share, flawed as I am, grew. And the world reminds me constantly that this stewardship takes place against a vicious social current, that nothing is guaranteed. I was gifted with children whose laughter surrounds like the scent of a May lilac bush, children who share the mien of God. But we are cursed with a cruel world. Such is life.

I am writing these words in the summer of 2018. We are in Japan, Kyoto specifically, where I am coteaching a

summer course on the history of a shared fascination between African Americans and Japanese people. I was first
in Japan when you were tiny. From the get-go there was
something about it that felt familiar in a genealogical way.
Farming is so present. Cultivators are everywhere. Cotton
garments, mostly blue and white, dry on clotheslines. Rust
and moisture are treated with patience. The elderly, often
shaped like the letter Q, faces craned upwards as their back-
bones bend towards the earth, ride bikes in silence. They
choose pedestrian or automobile rules as it suits them. Japan
is spare and luxurious at once. This is the first time you have
spent so long in a place with so few Black people. And yet,
the watchers are not everywhere. At least not in the same
way, with a predetermined assessment. We walk along the
street and the gazes we get are more furtive than they are
curious. The watching is deliberately not pronounced.

Japan is a place to contradict Virginia Woolf. Space is at
a premium. A room of one's own is a rarity. I write sitting on
my futon on the floor, my back to the wall, my feet stretched
out. The room is busy with our bags, and the feeling of ta-
tami on my heels is soothing. Light streams into curtainless
windows, and the buzz of the air purifier is intermittently
interrupted by the sound of the train, which travels until just
after midnight a block away.

Each day, in one way or another, I think about the basic
elements of a good life. Often when I am walking along

the Kamogawa River there are black cormorants swooping for catfish and fishermen with nets. The cranes are, like the black birds, solitary and lean, while the squat fat ducks with teal tucked into their sides wade together in packs. Water is noisy and the people mostly silent. This is abundance in a way that is only apparent when you are not on a treadmill towards too much. A good life includes a way to make a living that doesn't break your spirit. A place to gather, frequently, with friends and loved ones. Some leisure. Nourishment, adequate rest. A sense of purpose, which is a wildly variant thing, thank God. I want you to understand that is more than enough. It is everything. And yet, and of course this is easier for me to teach, I also want you to keep your vast imaginations, be wanderlustful for life. Passion is my preferred disposition, under a placid surface. Be hungry.

In Japan, each threshold is a cultivated experience. Entering is ceremonial. Crossing over, going inside or to the outside, is framed, a deliberate cultivation of wood and paint and shape. I peer through a vermillion temple gate, guarded by sleek stone foxes, and think: We are of a people who have stood at the vestibule. We are ever aware of the crossroads of life and death, native and stranger, spirit and flesh. Care for crossroads, even to the extent that you can literally see the geometry of each curve, the math of organic shapes, is so much of what enchants me about Japan, turns me inside out in the sweetest way. Nature is not opposition to that which is human made. Instead their intimacy, hideous and beautiful, is attended to. It is so different here, but it is a place that mirrors back what I know.

Maybe that isn't a contradiction.

The morning I learned about a little eight-year-old Black girl selling water in the US, I walked to buy you French pastries. A white woman, a weed entrepreneur, called the police on that little girl, a child who offered something sweet and refreshing in the heat. I was enraged. As I walked, a little boy, I think he was four or five, ran alongside me. He stopped and hopped, and made a roaring sound, his thick black hairs bouncing in unison. And then he ran again. At one point, he was underfoot. I stepped to the side to avoid him; we looked at each other and laughed hard. And then he kept running. I turned to catch eyes with his father. We smiled, he held his fingertips together and bowed slightly. I bowed back.

This is human. A simple pleasure, a fleeting generosity. The humor of whatever monsters that little boy was happily defeating. On the way back I stopped, as I often did, at the fruit stand run by an elderly woman. The cherries and nectarines were ripe yet firm. Sweet, crisp, and refreshing.

I sought out elders in Japan, as I do everywhere. They tend to be so kind. Like the man who handed you a cluster of berries, Issa, to feed the deer in Nara Park. You took them, with a bit of hesitation, and then delighted in the way the deer slurped them out of your hand. People had taught these deer, and Freeman, you learned it through fellowship with them, to bow. You bowed, the deer bowed, you handed them peanut butter–scented wafers, and they settled under the gentleness of your hands.

Who could call the police on a little girl offering sweet and refreshing water? What spirit of nastiness has to settle into a soul for that to happen? Not once, or twice, but thousands of times in some configuration or another in the United States. I am somewhat embarrassed at how happy I am to be away. To give my mind a break from the truth of our circumstance.

None of us speaks Japanese beyond a few words and phrases. Freeman, you immediately notice the American arrogance of that, the assumption—and it is fairly true—that we can come here without words at our disposal and navigate successfully. Traveling in a space with an unfamiliar language can be both nerve-wracking and comforting. We are spared, for six weeks, the racial coda of the American tongue, the chatter of cluelessness and the pressure upon our mouths to beat it back. In its place is our fascinated quiet at the hum around us. There are signs of Blackness everywhere: kimonos in Ankara prints, baseball caps pushed back, jazz clubs, and ambient percussiveness. I do not have a firm grasp on what is made of Blackness in the everyday. As in most of the world, I expect, there is an attribution of coolness to it and a circulation of the strange American cultural imperialism that makes fetish, desire, and revulsion into a neat package for consumption as if to say: Look, we still can trade the Negro for dollars and a good time. But that isn't everything. I know for sure. And in the unknown, in the curious prospect of discovery lies something we deeply want and need: possibility.

One evening, as I walk past a home bursting with the scent of lilies, I am intrigued with the possibility of fragrance gardening. Along the Kamogawa River, gardenias are planted, and when the breeze hits and the water crashes, the combination of scents is intoxicating. Although a lover of the visual beauty of flowers, I contemplate cultivating a garden for the dark. How would one do it? Night-blooming jasmine would be across the way from the tea roses. But the honeysuckle could be with the lilac and the jasmine; that would be intoxicating. And fir goes well with tuberose. What is musky in plant life? Maybe foxes would come to dance in heat, and that would meld smoothly. Imagine how beautiful and different it would be to make a garden of scent rather than sight . . . or maybe even sound. Does the wind travel through petals at varying frequencies? Can odor and resonance join to make melodies?

Angel Kyodo Williams, a Zen priest, a Black woman, of my generation, speaks of freeing oneself of the white mind, of its overwhelming method of seeing and interpreting, as a means of getting closer to truth. I must admit I am conflicted about the word "truth." Objectivity is more often a fiction than not. But I believe in what she says about how we ought to encounter life. She writes,

> If we are willing to accept truth just as it comes, without trying to change it to suit our needs, we become free of the anxiety that comes from the urge to change and control. By master I mean receive with our full minds, open and without resistance. It doesn't mean that you know everything. Rather, it means that you may not know anything at all in a situation, but you may have become so open to the infinite possibilities that you can approach and accept anything. Even pain.[3]

And even more significantly, love. In a life of authorship and interpretation, analysis and architecture and deconstruction, love is my cipher of choice. One that I have decided is better to have than the social contract or law sitting at your core, because you have entered it rather than simply being bound. It has its own improvisation and con-tingent rules and ethics. Some we give to our young; some they fashion from their own living. And they teach us in the process. They are doing so. Because every second-person sentence devoted to them in these pages is to all of us. It is received wisdom from their witness and passionate hope for their futures. We, you, they, do not have to fight a whole society over its terms to find another way of living as long as you love the right ones, freshly, and in the immediacy of your connection. And when you do fight, and I know you will, do not fear the humiliation of defeat. Defeat is not humiliating. Rather, passivity to evil is self-immolation. Witness the joy and the wound. Imagine and then create laughter and ideas and responsibility to one another. I know you are tired of old terrible people looking for you to save them, but the truth is we need you. We have made a disaster of things. We have failed our possibilities.

Find your tribe, the ones who speak your language, a bastard's tongue, no less beautiful than the King's English and instead much more so. The people with whom you can share the interior illumination, that is the sacramental bond. You may love everyone in an agape but hold yourself pre-cious for those few. Make in that love a technology to fill up the gaping holes, a gear that winds in the urgency of hope. It is from there that revolutionary possibility emerges. Avoid love affairs, romantic or platonic, that are bound to

acquire that certain emptiness born of tidy deferrals of longing, the sort of thing that conventions require. Instead, be
wildly courageous in all of your living. Not reckless, simply
courageous. The old folks used to say, Get your education;
they can't take that away from you. But what they really
can't take away is what learning, in its many forms, opens in
your mind and heart. And that is much more than formal
education. It is a way of living.

Issa, you came by this honestly. An extrovert, you feed
off connection with others. At around age six, you got in
my face, tired of my need to retreat into quiet, and yelled,
"Introverted is for when you are asleep!" While I watch the
beauty of the bonds you create with others, laughing and
running around together, I watch the beauty of the quiet
imagination of your brother, who often shares his care for
others in the form of drawings, photographs, and songs.
Your love is an exceeding sun. May all our lives remain in
the thick of it. Without a hard and fast gospel, but with
faith. And Freeman Diallo and Issa Garner.

Acknowledgments

I am grateful for and to my sons, Issa Garner Rabb and Freeman Diallo Perry Rabb, and to everyone who loves and teaches them, family and friends.

I am grateful for the entire Perry family and especially for my late grandmother Neida Garner Perry, who taught us that the children always come first.

I am grateful for the ancestors, including and especially those whose names I do not know and those whose words were never recorded.

Thank you to the entire Beacon Press community, especially my editor, Gayatri Patnaik, who envisioned this book.

Thank you to the Princeton African American Studies Department community.

Thank you to the students in the Japan Global Seminar: Japan and Black America: A Long Road of Discovery.

Notes

FEAR

1. June Jordan, "Poem About My Rights," in *Directed By Desire: The Collected Poems of June Jordan* (Port Townsend, WA: Copper Canyon Press, 2005).

2. Wole Soyinka, *Climate of Fear: The Quest for Dignity in a Dehumanized World* (New York: Random House, 2007), 10.

3. Matthew 6:34.

4. Ralph Waldo Emerson, *The Speaker: A Quarterly Magazine of Successful Readings* 7: 337.

5. Toni Cade Bambara, *Those Bones Are Not My Child: A Novel* (New York: Knopf Doubleday, 2009).

FLY

1. Ntozake Shange, *If I Can Cook/You Know God Can: African American Food Memories, Meditations, and Recipes* (1998; Boston: Beacon Press, 2019), 16–17.

2. Sylvia Plath, "Ariel," online at the Poetry Foundation website, https://www.poetryfoundation.org/poems/49001/ariel, accessed September 14, 2018.

3. Yusef Komunyakaa, "Blackberries," in *Magic City* (Middletown, CT: Wesleyan University Press, 1992), 27.

4. Marita Bonner, "On Being Young—a Woman—and Colored," in *Norton Anthology of African American Literature*, 3rd ed., ed. Henry Louis Gates Jr. and Valerie Smith (New York: W. W. Norton, 2014), 1245.

5. Ralph Ellison, "The Little Man at Chehaw Station," in *The Collected Essays of Ralph Ellison: Revised and Updated*, ed. John F. Callahan (New York: Random House, 2011), 495.

6. Richard Wright, *Native Son*, 1957 (New York: HarperCollins, 2009), 23.

7. Ralph Waldo Emerson, *The Heart of Emerson's Journals*, ed. Bliss Perry (New York: Dover Publications, 1937), 102.

8. "Leather from Human Skin," *Philadelphia News*, published in *Sacramento Daily Union*, November 12, 1887, https://cdnc.ucr.edu/cgi-bin/cdnc?a=d&d=SDU18871112.2.65.

FORTUNE

1. Derek Walcott, "The Antilles: Fragments of Epic Memory," Nobel Lecture, 1992, https://www.nobelprize.org/nobel_prizes/literature/laureates/1992/walcott-lecture.html, accessed August 1, 2018.

2. Gwendolyn Brooks, "Boy Breaking Glass," https://www.poetryfoundation.org/poems/43322/boy-breaking-glass, accessed August 1, 2018.

3. Samuel Taylor Coleridge, "The Rime of the Ancient Mariner Part II," Accredited Language Services, https://www.alsintl.com/resources/poetry/the-rime-of-the-ancient-mariner-part-ii/, accessed September 11, 2018.

4. Walter Burkert, "Oracles," *Greek Religion: Archaic and Classical*, trans. John Raffan, 1977 (Hoboken, NJ: Wiley, 2013), 8.3.

5. June Jordan, *Soulscript* (New York: Harlem Moon, 2004), 65.

AFTERWORD

1. Gabriel García Márquez, *Love in the Time of Cholera* (New York: Knopf, 1985), 328.

2. Dennis Brutus, "If This Life Is All We Have," Su'eddie in Life n' Literature, posted April 27, 2013, https://sueddie.wordpress.com/2013/04/27/if-this-life-is-all-we-have-a-poem-by-dennis-brutus.

3. Angel Kyodo Williams, *Being Black: Zen and the Art of Living with Fearlessness and Grace* (New York: Penguin, 2002).

About the Author

IMANI PERRY is the Hughes-Rogers Professor of African American Studies at Princeton University, where she also teaches in the Programs in Law and Public Affairs, and Gender and Sexuality Studies. Perry, who holds a BA from Yale University and a PhD in American studies and law degree from Harvard University, is a native of Birmingham, Alabama, and spent much of her youth in Cambridge, Massachusetts, and Chicago. She is the author of six books, including the 2019 NAACP Image Award nominee *May We Forever Stand: A History of the Black National Anthem*, *Vexy Thing: On Gender and Liberation*, and *Looking for Lorraine: The Radiant and Radical Life of Lorraine Hansberry*, which won the 2019 PEN/Jacqueline Bograd Weld Award for Biography and was a *New York Times* Notable Book of 2018. She lives outside Philadelphia with her two sons, Freeman Diallo Perry Rabb and Issa Garner Rabb.